Before "I Do"

Before "I Do"

Anthony Garascia

Preparing for the Sacrament of Marriage

ave maria press   Notre Dame, Indiana

Anthony Garascia currently serves as a pastoral minister and marriage and family therapist at St. Pius X Parish in Granger, Indiana. He holds an M.A. in Liturgical Studies from Catholic University and an M.S. in Counseling from Indiana University. In addition to his pastoral work, he serves as an adjunct faculty member in the theology department at the University of Notre Dame. His articles have appeared in numerous journals, including *Today's Parish, Living Light, Catechumenate,* and *Worship.*

Nihil obstat: Rev. Augustine DiNoia, O.P.; Mr. Fred Everett, Mrs. Lisa Everett; Rev. Jerome Listecki; Rev. Val Peter; Daniel Scheidt; Prof. Janet Smith; Rev. Peter Uglietto.

Imprimatur: Most Rev. John M. D'Arcy
Bishop of Fort Wayne-South Bend
November 1, 1998, Feast of All Saints

The *Imprimatur* is an official declaration that a book or pamphlet is free of doctrinal or moral error. No implication is contained therein that those who have granted the *Imprimatur* agree with its contents, opinions, or statements expressed.

© 1999 by Ave Maria Press, Inc.

International Standard Book Number: 0-87793-660-9

Cover and text design by Brian C. Conley

Printed and bound in the United States of America.

Library of Congress Cataloging-in-Publication Data
Garascia, Anthony
      Before "I do" : preparing for the sacrament of marriage / Anthony Garascia.
            p.   cm.
      Includes bibliographical references.
      ISBN 0-87793-660-9
      1. Marriage—Religious aspects—Catholic Church. 2. Catholic Church—Doctrines. 3. Married people—Religious life. 4. Catholic Church—Membership.   I. Title.
      BX2250.G356   1998
      259'.13—dc21 98-23880
                                                  CIP

To Beth—
friend, spouse, lover:
You have taught me more than
you'll ever know about life,
marriage, and faith.

Contents

Introduction

Marriage, like life, is a journey that involves the totality of a person. In that journey we partner with another person and pledge to share our innermost thoughts, lie in a common bed, become best friends, resolve conflict when it arises, and strive for happiness together. This journey has many unforeseen twists and detours, and while the journey is exciting and full of promise, it can also be scary and frightening.

The journey of marriage is a journey of faith—in ourselves, our abilities, our future, and most importantly in the unseen God who walks with us down the road we travel. In this journey we discover the mystery of ourselves. We come to realize that our relationship brings to the surface aspects of ourselves that have lain dormant and hidden. We find hidden strengths, and yes, we often find hidden, sinful patterns that we didn't realize were there when we began the journey. But we also find the hidden but ever-present God who resides within us, inhabiting both the places of light and of darkness.

The Church calls marriage a "vocation." This means that marriage is the journey by which we achieve holiness, find God, and cooperate with the Holy Spirit in transforming the world into the best possible likeness of the kingdom of God that Jesus proclaimed. In marriage the ordinary experiences of everyday intimacy and conflict reveal our capacity for good and evil. Yet it is the graced, intentional commitment to finding God that takes a Christian couple beyond themselves and points them toward the people they are destined to be: sinners called to holiness and wholeness. Marriage, in short, is a journey in which we achieve, through the grace of God, holiness and wholeness.

Whenever one embarks on a serious journey, planning and imagination are required. Planning is required for all the things that we will need during the journey, and imagination in order to construct a spiritual road map that tells us how to get where we want to go.

Before you embark on this preparation program use your imagination a bit and read the following adaptation of a journey story from the Gospel of Luke:

> It was the day following the Sabbath, the first day of the week. Two people, a husband and wife, were hurrying back to a small town named Emmaus. They had made a pilgrimage to Jerusalem for the high holy days of Passover, and now they were eager to return to their village.

They were eager for more than the usual reasons, for they had witnessed an incredible event while in Jerusalem. A man named Jesus, with a reputation as a prophet and healer, had been put to death. What made this an incredible event for them was that they had met the man briefly some two years ago in a small village named Cana. They had traveled there as a betrothed couple to attend a wedding of a friend. All had gone as expected until an awkward moment at the wedding banquet: someone had apparently forgotten to order enough wine, and the bride and groom were in danger not only of embarrassment, but shame. Then, almost as soon as the commotion started, it subsided. Wine suddenly flowed, and there was a murmur in the crowd that a person named Jesus had somehow provided wine for the banquet. Some called it a miracle; others marveled at the turn of good luck; still others were just happy that the party wouldn't be breaking up after all. As for the engaged couple, they marveled at the event and began to listen more to the "good news" that this man Jesus had talked about. Eventually, they became his followers and would, from time to time, travel to where he was staying to hear him speak of the law and prophets.

Now, two years later, this Jesus had been crucified, and the couple journeying back from Emmaus had trouble understanding why. As they walked they spoke intently of the events that had happened, and before long a stranger approached them and asked if he could walk with them. Accepting him into their small traveling party the husband and wife told him what had happened in the last three days—of the trial, the condemnation to death, and the crucifixion of Jesus.

All three were absorbed in the discussion. As evening approached they looked for lodging and found a small inn. The stranger said at first that he would go on, but the couple pressed him to stay and dine with them. He agreed, and they found a table around which they had food and wine set. As a sign of hospitality the two asked the stranger to say a blessing over the bread. As he spoke the words of blessing, another incredible thing happened to them: they had a sense of déjà vu, almost as if the man Jesus was present in the room. On coming out of their daze they found that the stranger had vanished. They immediately recognized the presence of Jesus, and in their excitement got up from the table and hurried back to Jerusalem to tell others that they had seen him. . . .

Now, some fifteen years later, the married couple that recognized Jesus in the breaking of the bread are grandparents. They look at a wonderful extended family and know that God has blessed them. They are also leaders in the local church in Jerusalem and have convened their own "house church" where fellow Christians gather to tell the stories of Jesus and participate in the breaking of the bread. Both of them, in their own ways, have done what they could to help those less fortunate and witness to the truth as they saw it. Their early journey of marriage was transformed and redirected by their encounter with the risen Christ on the road to Emmaus.

The above imaginative story is based on Luke 24:13-35. We have become accustomed to speaking about disciples of Christ apart from their lived situation. Maybe the two people on the road to Emmaus were not a married couple, but suppose they were. We can well imagine that their own lives, and their marriage, would have been transformed by such an event. Their own purpose for living, and the structure of their marriage, would have been redirected and re-energized by meeting the risen Christ.

Is there any application of this imaginative story for marriage today? If marriage is a graced reality, shouldn't we expect stories like the above to happen? How would your own marriage be different and unfold differently if you opened yourselves up to imagine that your journey was part of a larger unfolding journey, a journey where we all walk in pilgrimage toward a better world proclaimed by Jesus?

How would your marriage be different if you believed firmly that the way the two of you live your married life matters to the future of the world? It will certainly matter to any of your future children. Whatever the answer, it is yours to plan and imagine your future together. May God walk with you as you do!

1

Building Your Marriage on a Sound Foundation

Welcome to *Before "I Do"*! As your wedding date draws ever closer, we hope that this session will help you get in touch with the original excitement and love that brought you and your fiancé to the decision of marriage. We invite you to reflect, individually and together, on your own expectations concerning marriage and the Church's expectations and hopes for you. You are also invited to consider the foundations of a healthy and lasting marriage.

1. So Much Energy, So Much Excitement

When two people marry, one often finds a great amount of energy and excitement. Marriage ceremonies and receptions are fun and happy events because they are opportunities for both of your families and your friends to come together to celebrate something they all have in common: their affirmation and love for you as you pledge your love and fidelity to one another. People often travel from great distances to be with the newly married couple, and seeing one's friends and family gather to celebrate with you can be an overwhelming experience. A newly married person described her wedding day this way:

> The entire day was great! We had put so much energy into planning the wedding itself, and to see our many friends and family members come together and help us celebrate was awesome. We were given many compliments on the wedding itself, but the thing that I remember the most was the presence of many of our good friends who were there with us. Someone mentioned to me that this is what life in heaven must be like: people gathered together, everyone happy, friends having reunions with people they haven't seen for so long, singing, dancing, eating, and yes, some drinking. I was so happy at the end of the day and will remember all of this for the rest of my life.

It comes as no surprise that the image of the wedding feast is one of the major images used in scriptures to describe the kingdom of God. When searching for a way to describe the love affair between God and humanity the authors of the various books of the Bible were inspired by the Spirit to use the image of marriage. This is because of the love, intimacy, respect, and fidelity present in sound marriages. We can also remind ourselves that in the Gospel of John, Jesus begins his ministry at the wedding at Cana.

Put simply, married love can and often does point to the mystery of God's continuing love for humanity and for the covenant relationship that exists between God and his people. Married love also points toward the energy and creative power of the Spirit of God; one instinctively thinks of the awesome mystery of bringing children into the world. In fact, our word for this comes close to the creative act of God: we say we "procreate"—with the help of God's Spirit we co-create by bringing children into the world. Without often realizing it, married people share in the task of pointing toward the presence of God working in the world. This is what the Church means when it describes marriage as a sacrament.

Marriage is both a sign and an instrument of the communion that God shares with us.

"*The vocation to marriage is written in the very nature of man and woman as they came from the hand of the Creator*" (Catechism of the Catholic Church #1603).

Reflecting Together

As you begin this marriage preparation experience, it is important to tap the energy and excitement that defines your commitment thus far. Take some time to complete the following questions about your early courtship and falling in love.

What I remember about our first meeting is . . .

My first impressions of you were . . .

I knew that I was in love with you when . . .

The one thing I want you to know about me concerning our being married is . . .

If our marriage commitment symbolizes anything, I want people to see . . .

2. The Gifts We Give

Another exciting thing about getting married is the many gifts that a couple receives. While many of these gifts are material in nature, others may be gifts of time, caring, or presence. Over time some of these gifts will come to symbolize your marriage commitment.

> One couple remembers the gift of an earthenware bowl that was made in the Southwest. Throughout the years that bowl was used for many different dishes and sustained numerous falls and breaks. Each time the break was repaired with a strong bonding glue. In time it became a symbol of the couple's own marriage and its ability to sustain the various blows to its structure that are a normal part of a marriage.

As you prepare for marriage it is important to affirm that you are a gift to your spouse-to-be, just as Christ gave himself to the world. And while you will give each other many material gifts over the course of your marriage, the most important gifts are the intangible ones that often go unnamed.

Take a few moments to identify the most important gifts that you give each other. There are twelve gifts listed below. Prioritize the gifts in order of importance, placing a "1" next to the most important gift and so on down the list. Be sure to list any other gifts that you consider a high priority as you begin your marriage.

As we begin our married life I give you the gift of . . .

_____ Admiring you

_____ Validating your feelings

_____ Being there for you

_____ Listening to you

_____ Spending time with you

_____ Being honest with you

_____ Touching you tenderly, holding you

_____ Believing what you say

_____ Encouraging you

_____ Making passionate love to you

_____ Telling you when I am hurt

_____ Being open to change throughout our marriage

_____ Other:

3. Your Expectations

All of us bring into our marriage a set of expectations concerning how our needs will be met and how we will love each other. One married man expressed his expectations in this way: In marriage I want . . .

Happiness	Admiration for things I do
Love	Great sex life
Trust	To be best friends
Affection	

Write your own list of expectations for your marriage. Include any of the above and others not listed.

In marriage I want . . .

4. Great Expectations

Just as you do, the Church has great expectations for your married life. We expect that the love you have for one another will not only express your lived commitment, but it will point towards a deeper mystery of God's love for the world. That is why we call the marriage of two baptized Christians a sacrament.

When we face a lifetime commitment we may feel overwhelmed about our ability to guarantee that we can deliver on our promises and expectations. Our world changes so rapidly, and none of us can foresee what the future holds. But if you have any fear about your commitment, remember that in the end it is the grace of God that sustains our commitments and creates possibilities out of seemingly impossible obstacles. If we do our part by taking care of the work of intimacy and commitment, then we can trust that God will sustain our efforts.

5. Realistic Expectations?

We can, however, bring beliefs and expectations about our marriage that are impossible to fulfill and that can cause a great deal of frustration and pain. Spend some time in reacting to the following set of expectations.

I will meet all of his or her needs. She or he will meet all of my needs.

Makes sense: ❑   Not sure I agree with this: ❑

You can help your fiancé meet his or her needs, but the responsibility for this begins with him or her. There are some needs that we have that are unique to ourselves. One fiancé might prefer to relax by running ten miles; it could be unrealistic for the other to be expected to tag along with him or her. What is more realistic is giving our fiancé affirmation to meet his or her needs once they are voiced.

Comments:

In a marriage there are just "his or her" needs and my needs.

Makes sense: ❑   Not sure I agree with this: ❑

In fact, when you marry each other, you create a third entity entitled "the relationship." It needs caring and feeding. It also has needs which, if neglected, will cause your marriage to suffer. There are three areas of need in a marriage: your needs, my needs, and our needs. The relationship speaks to our needs. So, add to the discussion of "How do I help you meet your needs?" these questions: "What do we do to care for our relationship? How do we nurture our relationship?"

Comments:

Marriage will change my fiancé.

Makes sense: ❏   Not sure I agree with this: ❏

Not necessarily. Marriage often changes us, but only because we consent to the change. In the beginning change is fun. But then, after some time, we come to those parts of us that are pretty ingrained, like stubbornness, tendencies to anger, tendencies to procrastinate, and the like. Also, there might be deeper issues that have been masked by the initial happiness of courtship, like being depressed or having a tendency to drink too much. (Sometimes these tendencies appear to be "under control" during courtship.) These issues may sometimes prompt us to say, "If you loved me you would change." The more profound statement that each partner must make is: "I love you so much that I will take responsibility to confront the unfinished and possibly hurting parts of myself and, if necessary, change."

Comments:

I'm responsible for my fiancé's happiness.

Makes sense: ❏   Not sure I agree with this: ❏

This is related to the two previous statements. Happiness involves an exterior and interior framework. What goes on outside of me does influence my happiness to a degree and my fiancé is a part of that picture. But the interior frame is the most important. That is the area of my personal decision to strive for happiness. This is often related to my own self-esteem and how I feel about myself. Often, when our esteem is low, we look for people on the outside to build it up. Then, if we don't feel good, we blame them. If I decide to avoid happiness, then nothing my fiancé says or does will make me happy. The inner work of happiness is my task.

Comments:

I don't have to tell my fiancé that I love her or him. She or he will just know.

Makes sense: ❏   Not sure I agree with this: ❏

Dr. John Gottmann is a marriage researcher who has studied couples for some twenty years. He has come up with what he describes as the "five-to-one" rule: for every negative exchange between the couple there needs to be five positive exchanges that counteract the affects of the negative one. This means two things: that we are more sensitive to negative exchanges, and that we need to make an effort to give the other positive feedback. We actually tell our fiancé we love him or her by maintaining the five-to-one rule.

Comments:

If we truly love each other we will not get angry with each other.

Makes sense: ❏   Not sure I agree with this: ❏

We tend to have a love/hate relationship with the feeling of anger. On the one hand we fear being negated and put down by a loved one's anger. We may have experienced this in our own families. On the other hand, we use anger to help us express our feelings when things are unfair or wrong in our lives. A wise person once commented that anger and conflict can be "holy ground" on which we grow deeper. Have you ever thought of anger as a potentially holy thing? It can be, as long as we have worked out the rules of conflict that we will use in our marriage.

Comments:

My fiancé knows what I want without my telling him or her.

Makes sense: ❏   Not sure I agree with this: ❏

This is another variation on the business of meeting and expressing needs. Marriage is all about communication, and one of the cardinal sins that married couples commit is that of "mind reading." We often think we know what the other wants or is thinking, but until we check this out with the other we can never be quite sure. The reverse is also true: my fiancé can only guess at what I want if I don't take responsibility for communication. Acting on assumptions in a relationship is a sure way of creating an argument.

Comments:

It's not all that important to work out household duties and responsibilities.

Makes sense: ❏   Not sure I agree with this: ❏

The same researcher, Dr. John Gottmann, found that in marriages where men participated more equally in household chores there was a much higher level of satisfaction. It is important to talk about household duties and responsibilities because of the potential resentment that can emerge if one spouse feels he or she is carrying the brunt of the work.

Comments:

Having consensus on religious beliefs and practices is not important.

Makes sense: ❏   Not sure I agree with this: ❏

Studies have shown that couples who have resolved the question of religious belief and practice have reduced tension in their relationship. Some studies suggest that those people who attend church on a regular basis report having more satisfaction and actually live longer. So, while this might not be high on your list right now, it will become more important later on in your marriage, especially when you have children.

Comments:

We don't need to budget our money. Because we love each other we'll be able to handle this.

Makes sense: ❏   Not sure I agree with this: ❏

Actually, because you love each other it makes sense not to let budget expectations and differences come between the two of you. Common agreement on household finances can only minimize the potential for tension down the line. It's possible that each of you have specific interests and activities that involve spending money that the other person doesn't share. For instance, suppose one of you wants to spend $20 every week playing golf. That is not necessarily a bad thing, but it can lead to increased tension if you don't identify your specific expectations concerning budgeting and spending of money.

Comments:

See the chart entitled "Money and Our Budget" on the next page.

Money and Our Budget

INCOME	
His Monthly Income:	
Her Monthly Income:	
Total Monthly Income:	

FIXED EXPENSES: Estimate where needed	MONTH ONE	MONTH TWO	MONTH THREE	MONTH FOUR	MONTH FIVE	MONTH SIX
Housing (Mortgage/Rent)						
Clothing						
Life Insurance						
Car Payments						
Car Upkeep (not including fuel)						
Fuel, Car						
Heating and Electric						
Groceries and Food						
Telephone						
Credit Card Debt						
Pharmacy						
Medical, Doctor						
Dental						
Contributions to Charity						
Home Maintenance						
Gifts						
Hobbies						
Entertainment						
IRA, Retirement						
Vacations						
His Monthly Money						
Her Monthly Money						
Savings						
Miscellaneous						
Other						
Total Monthly Income						
Total Estimated Expenses						
Is there a surplus or deficit?	If deficit, what can be cut back?					

In the space below list as many things as you can that you enjoy doing. The list can include things like shopping, going to movies, going out to lunch, etc. After you have the list completed go over and prioritize the items on your list starting with the most important. Then, estimate how much money you will need to do this activity on a monthly basis. This will give you a rough idea of how much money you each will spend a month on personal needs.

His Needs/Wants

Her Needs/Wants

6. Building the House of Your Marriage on Solid Ground

In the Gospel of Luke Jesus compares the wise disciple to the builder of a house "who dug deeply and laid the foundation on rock; when the flood came, the river burst against that house but could not shake it because it had been well built" (Lk 7:48). The task of marriage is much the same: as architects and builders you are given the opportunity to build your marriage on a firm foundation, one that can withstand not only earthquakes, but also floods. Whatever the crisis, taking some time to focus on your foundation right now is good insurance against unexpected trouble in the future.

In the earthquake-prone parts of California, new homes and office buildings are constructed to withstand the incredible force of the earth. Foundations are build in such a way not only to withstand the quaking earth, but in many cases to absorb and distribute the energy of a quake so that the potential damage to the structure is minimized. Much thought and planning has gone into the design of these structures, because once the foundation is undermined by a quake the only thing left to do is to tear down the whole building and start over.

Marriage today is something like building a house in a quake-prone area. We know that there are forces out there that can pull apart the foundations of a marriage. In dangerous times, well-constructed spiritual, psychological and physical foundations go a long way in helping us weather unexpected troubles. It's not that we go looking for trouble, but if we live long enough trouble of some sort—whether it be unemployment, sickness, death of a loved one, or more—will find us.

In order to sustain the impact of earthquakes, buildings are constructed so that they sway with the shock waves of the earth. A well-built structure has built-in flexibility, enabling it to provide safety for its occupants in times of trouble. Building the house of your marriage is much the same: your marriage needs to have a type of "sway" or flexible resiliency that can roll with the shock waves of the unexpected intrusion.

That is why it is important for you to define the foundational values and practices that can guide you not only through the good times, but also the times of trouble. You can think of these values as a personal mission statement that reminds you of your identity and purpose. They will see you through, even when you feel as if the ground is shaking beneath you.

Reflecting Together

1. Whom do you look to right now as an example of a couple with a successful marriage? What qualities does their marriage possess that you admire?

2. If you were giving advice to someone getting married about what it takes to be married successfully, what four or five things would you tell them to work on?

7. Twelve Foundational Factors That Form a Healthy Marriage

The following factors have been gleaned from three sources: the tradition of the Church, research in the social sciences concerning marriage, and the experience of couples who have been successfully married for many years. If you pay attention to them through the years, the odds are you will achieve happiness. They are arranged in four sets and represent four pillars on which a strong, yet flexible, foundation rests.

Take some time to consider the following foundational factors, compare them with the factors you have already articulated in the reflection questions above, and answer the reflection questions concerning each value.

Friendship Factors

These factors form the glue that holds the relationship together from beginning to end.

Love: a feeling, but more than a feeling; a process of being united that expresses the mystery and uniqueness of companionship lived over a lifetime.

Can you name two or three things you do to in a typical week to show your fiancé love and affection?

How were love and affection expressed in your own family? Were there any difficulties in this area?

Respect: the esteeming and honoring of someone as a unique person; a recognition that my fiancé represents the embodiment of God's presence for me, and that I honor him or her as a temple of God's Spirit. This recognition means that there is no place for physical violence and/or speech that belittles and intimidates. Respect requires me to recognize anger as a feeling and not as a means of controlling or retaliating against another.

For what do you respect your fiancé right now? Be as specific as possible: list qualities, factors, behaviors.

Did you feel that you counted in your family growing up? Would you say that you have "low," "medium," or "high" self-esteem right now?

Honesty: the honoring of my own integrity so that I tell the truth as I see it in a spirit of sincerity and charity, seeking the betterment of myself and my fiancé. Honesty serves as a spiritual "curative" since it cuts through denial to the truth.

> Do you have an easy or difficult time being honest about what you are feeling or thinking? If you have difficulty, what stops you from an honest sharing?

High-Touch Factors

These factors speak to the reality that we are people who are a unique combination of mind and body. These factors also allow the married couple to explore their own bodies in a spirit of safety and passion whereby the love of God becomes present in a truly Christian manner.

Intimacy: The passionate creation of emotional and sexual closeness that says: "I have let you discover my innermost core; few others, perhaps no one, have been there but you. I have discovered your innermost core and there have found the presence of God."

> Are there any blocks to creating intimacy between you and your fiancé that, if talked about now, could make your marriage stronger?

> Will you feel comfortable sharing with each other what gives you sexual pleasure? Will this be difficult or easy to talk about?

Communication: the learning and sharing of a common language and vocabulary that will help direct the marriage; problem-solving, but more than just words: risk-taking, the sharing of feelings and emotional states. This means a commitment to resolving disputes in a nonviolent manner.

> In the course of your relationship so far, have you taken any risks with your fiancé in order to solve a problem between the two of you? How would you describe the risk you took?

Trust/Fidelity: true passion, emotional and sexual, cannot take place without a circle of safety. Trust/Fidelity creates that framework and says: "I will honor you by not seeking passion and intimacy outside this circle. I may have friends, but not on the same level of communication and intimacy I share with you."

> Has mutual trust been there from the beginning of your relationship? How do you and your fiancé build trust in each other? What do you do or say to ensure that trust is present?

> How do the two of you handle the issue of having separate friends? Has this caused any tension so far where you have had to talk things through? Describe the process.

Transcendent Factors

These factors speak to a person having to "stretch" or transcend himself or herself. These factors often take us out of our normal selves and may move into compassion and empathy for others.

Prayer/Spirituality: a perspective that is open to the mystery of God, of others, and of myself; a prayerful, spiritual disposition enables us to face the ultimate mysteries of suffering and death.

> What common religious practices did your own family have?

> What common religious practices, if any, do you expect to have as a married couple?

> What role will participation in the Church's sacramental life, especially the Eucharist, play in your marriage?

Forgiveness: the letting-go or giving-up of resentment toward another; forgiveness often requires a letting-go of our anger. Seeking forgiveness is the other side of the coin. Can I move beyond my hurt and stubbornness to forgive and seek forgiveness?

> Is forgiveness an easy or difficult thing for you? Has there ever been a time when you forgave someone for betraying your trust? How did that happen?

> Have you considered celebrating the sacrament of reconciliation as part of your preparation for marriage?

Community: this value speaks to how a couple is connected to family, friends, church, and other organizations. It also speaks to how, and in what way, the couple is of service to the larger world beyond themselves.

> If your marriage was ever in trouble, which family members or friends would you turn to? Which organizations (parish, counseling agencies) would you to turn to?

Flexibility Factors

These factors address how resilient a marriage is in facing the unexpected bumps and bruises that life dishes out. They provide the foundation of a marriage with "shock absorbers" that help the marriage withstand the earthquakes that sometimes hit without notice. They help the structure of your marriage sway rather than crumble.

Humor: a sense of humor is important for a marriage. It can be helpful sometimes to laugh at our predicaments; humor helps us transcend anxiety and pain. However, humor can also be a way of avoiding problems if the other factors listed above are not present. Jokes at the expense of the other—sarcasm, teasing, and the like—are not really humor but can be expressions of thinly disguised anger at the other person.

> Did members of your own family possess a sense of humor? Were jokes ever aimed at an individual family member? Which family member do you admire most for his or her sense of humor?

Perseverance: the ability to hang in there with adversity rather than to "cut and run" when the going gets tough. This value often leads the couple to seek counseling for problems that seem unsolvable. It is the attitude that says, "I'll do whatever I need to in order to make my marriage better."

Is there a person or married couple that models for you the value of hanging in there when the going gets tough? Describe the qualities that impress you.

Do you have the right amount of perseverance or is this a value that you would like more of?

Adaptability: the ability to change when the situation calls for it. This involves a commitment to work on any unfinished business from my childhood that might get in the way of deepening my marriage commitment.

When thinking of your own family growing up, were your parents more or less adaptable to the many demands of life and family? Who do you look to as someone able to change when it is necessary to do so?

Case Study 1

Todd and Angie have been married for six years and have three small children, ages one, three, and five. Angie works part-time for a local high school; Todd is a construction manager. Together they make a comfortable income. When they were dating Todd and Angie often met friends at a local sports bar. While they drank, their drinking was seldom abusive or a problem. Also, sometimes they would smoke marijuana with friends, usually on the weekends.

When they started their family, Angie decided to forgo the occasional smoking of marijuana and both frequented the bar scene less and less. What Angie didn't realize was that Todd developed a pattern of stopping after work with some of his friends for a drink or two. About a year ago she became aware of this pattern and raised her concerns with Todd. There continued to be tension over this issue. As Angie feared, the pattern developed into a full-blown crisis. Todd was pulled over by a policeman and charged with driving under the influence of alcohol. But there was more. The police found a small amount of cocaine in the car, and Todd was arrested. Since this was his first offense, the court gave Todd a choice: jail time or entry into a treatment program.

For her part Angie felt that the very core of their marriage was threatened. She made it clear to Todd that she wanted to work on the marriage, but that Todd needed to make a basic decision to abstain from alcohol and other drugs, and to give the marriage top priority. At first it wasn't easy: four weeks of intensive out-patient treatment, a family-and-marriage program, and then a recommendation of aftercare where Todd was strongly encouraged to attend Narcotics Anonymous and Angie, Al-Anon. Angie feared that Todd's commitment to the twelve-step group would waver in time. But it didn't. Todd refocused his energy and found a certain spiritual renewal in adopting new ways of thinking, feeling, and acting.

Todd's recovery has been underway now for some twelve years. He attends a weekly twelve-step group. Together, he and Angie formed new, healthier friendships where drinking was not a central activity. They also became more involved in their local parish community and each has their own volunteer activities where they give their time and energy. They both look back to Todd's arrest as a turning point for their marriage, a re-choosing of the underlying foundations of their marriage.

Reflecting Together

1. Do you know anyone who has gone through a similar honest, yet painful, appraisal of the condition of their marriage where the outcome has been positive?

2. In the above case Angie was honest with Todd about where she stood concerning the marriage and called him to be honest with himself. Do you think she did the right thing to ask Todd to make a choice to abstain from the use of alcohol and other drugs so as to focus on the marriage? Why or why not?

3. Do you see the above case as a spiritual crisis for Todd and Angie?

4. When a couple makes their wedding vows, do you think this implies a willingness to work through whatever problems may emerge? When you think of the resources that you outlined in the beginning of this section, which ones would you fall back on to help you make it through (if you were in Todd and Angie's shoes)?

Case Study 2

Gail and Tim had been engaged for a year, both of them just finishing up their undergraduate degrees. Tim had studied electrical engineering in the army and had continued in this direction through his college years. Gail had pursued a degree in education with plans to teach after college. Before they were engaged they had dated steadily with the understanding that they would not date anyone else unless they had first talked about this. The period of "steady dating" overlapped with Tim's last year in the service and continued after he was discharged.

Just recently Tim revealed to Gail that while he was in the army he did not keep his pledge of being exclusive, and that he had on several occasions dated other women. Upon further questioning and prodding by Gail, he admitted that he had been sexually intimate with another woman.

Gail was hurt and torn by Tim's confession. On the one hand she understood Tim's situation and was glad for his honesty. On the other hand she felt that Tim had been unfaithful to their agreement. She was further worried because she knew that Tim's own father had had a series of affairs while married, which contributed to Tim's parents divorcing. As a result of her concerns she asked Tim to go into pre-marital counseling with her. She was uncertain as to whether she should postpone the wedding (some eleven months away). After all, she loved Tim and wanted to believe him that this was a "one-time thing" brought about by his being isolated and alone on an army base. Some of her friends had advised her to "call it off right away," but she couldn't just walk away from what she felt was the right relationship for her.

Reflecting Together

1. If you were Tim's best friend, how would you advise him? If you were Gail's best friend, how would you advise her?

2. What has to happen in order for Gail to feel more trusting and move beyond her hurt? With the marriage eleven months away, do you think they have enough time to work this through?

3. Do you think Gail's fear that Tim's behavior might represent a pattern, not just an isolated event, is justified? Would it concern you that Tim's father had a history of affairs?

2

The Two Will Become One

In this session you will reflect on the task of separating from your own family and accepting the responsibility to join together to create a new home. Although we may not customarily think of marriage as a group of tasks to be performed, a successful marriage does involve achieving certain goals and accomplishing certain tasks. The first step in this task is to realize that marriage creates a new psychological and spiritual reality. At the beginning of this venture it is important for you to identify those specific areas of your personal life that will help you accomplish this task and those that possibly will hinder its completion. This session begins with a brief reflection on the faith dimension of marriage.

1. Faith at the Heart of Your Marriage

As Christians, we believe that marriage embodies Christ's love through the love of husband and wife. In other words, the married couple brings the presence of God to the world though the unique way they live in relationship with each other. Christian marriage participates in what can be described as the "incarnational principle." Our belief in the incarnation teaches us that in Jesus, God embraces the human condition and knows our joys, fears, sufferings, triumphs, and defeats in an intimate way. In a sense, married people carry on the grace of the incarnation by making real the presence of God—to each other and in the world.

We Catholic Christians believe that through the grace of God we have the means to live our lives to their fullest potential. When this occurs we experience a deep unity between us and God. This reminds us of the mystery of Christ in whom humanity and divinity form a perfect unity. It is Christ that brings us to God; he serves as a bridge between ourselves and God.

In the sacrament of marriage the Church believes that a similar unity is possible. The man and woman unite in their love for one another. This marital love, however, has its foundations in Christ, who loved humanity so much that he gave his life. Marital love, because it is sacramental, points to the love that God has for the world. Just as Christ closes the gap between God and humanity, so too does married love when it witnesses to the presence of Christ. In a sense the two married spouses become Christ for one another, and their love for one another bears a quiet yet powerful witness to the love that Christ has for the Church and the world.

St. Paul expressed the mystery of marriage this way:

> Husbands, love your wives, as Christ loved the church. He gave himself up for her to make her holy, purifying her in the bath of water by the power of the word, to present to himself a glorious church, holy and immaculate, without stain or wrinkle or anything of that sort. Husbands should love their wives as they do their own bodies. He who loves his wife loves himself. Observe that no one ever hates his own flesh; no, he nourishes it and takes care of it as Christ cares for the church—for we are members of his body.

> "For this reason a man shall leave his father and mother, and shall cling to his wife, and the two shall be made into one." This is a great foreshadowing; I mean that it refers to Christ and the church. In any case, each one should love his wife as he loves himself, the wife for her part showing respect for her husband (Eph 5:25-32, NAB).

Reflecting Together

1. React to this thought: The way you and your fiancé relate together and love each other makes real the love that Christ has for the Church and the world.

❏ I'm impressed   ❏ I need to think about this

❏ I'm confused   ❏ I'm honored by the responsibility

❏ That's a lot of responsibility   ❏ Other thoughts:

2. St. Paul indicates that the call or vocation to Christian marriage is rooted in the love and respect that Christ has for the Church. Can you name one or two things that you did this last week to show love and respect for your fiancé?

3. If a couple really believes that the way they relate to each other makes real the love that Christ has for the Church and the world, how would they act differently toward one another?

4. Do you know any couples who you admire for the way they love and respect each other? What qualities do they exhibit that you admire? Have you ever thought of them making present the love of God by the way they treated each other?

Since God created him man and woman, their mutual love becomes an image of the absolute and unfailing love with which God loves man. It is good, very good, in the Creator's eyes. And this love which God blesses is intended to be fruitful and to be realized in the common work of watching over creation: "And God blessed them and God said to them: 'Be fruitful and multiply, and fill the earth and subdue it'" (Catechism of the Catholic Church #1604).

2. Knowing Yourself

As you strive to create this new identity as a married couple you need to know who you are and how you have been formed by your own families of origin. The exercises below will help you become aware of what you bring into your marriage commitment.

I'm the type of person who . . . (Place your initial in the space indicating your response.)

Knows the difference between a dinner fork and a salad fork.

___ Yes   ___ No   ___ Uncertain

Prefers a quiet evening talking with friends to a party with dancing and music.

___ Yes   ___ No   ___ Uncertain

Puts a hundred-and-ten percent into whatever I do.

___ Yes   ___ No   ___ Uncertain

Likes to follow conventional ways of doing things over the experimental and unconventional.

___ Yes   ___ No   ___ Uncertain

Expresses my feelings immediately when something upsets me.

___ Yes   ___ No   ___ Uncertain

Is confident most of the time.

___ Yes   ___ No   ___ Uncertain

Is considered by those who know me as calm and reliable.

___ Yes   ___ No   ___ Uncertain

Is more reserved than affectionate.

___ Yes   ___ No   ___ Uncertain

Is more of a spender than a saver.

___ Yes   ___ No   ___ Uncertain

Sometimes struggles with low self-esteem.

___ Yes   ___ No   ___ Uncertain

Is competitive in most things I do.

___ Yes   ___ No   ___ Uncertain

Squeezes the toothpaste tube in the middle.

___ Yes   ___ No   ___ Uncertain

Likes to keep a neat office or room with everything in its place.

___ Yes   ___ No   ___ Uncertain

Likes to be spontaneous when making plans.

___ Yes   ___ No   ___ Uncertain

Would be the first to talk or contribute in a discussion group.

___ Yes   ___ No   ___ Uncertain

Gets angry with myself when things go wrong.

___ Yes   ___ No   ___ Uncertain

Tries to get people to cooperate and get along.

___ Yes   ___ No   ___ Uncertain

Can get pretty intense when I have a problem that really concerns me.

___ Yes   ___ No   ___ Uncertain

Is more of a "thinker" than a "feeler."

___ Yes   ___ No   ___ Uncertain

Is usually late for most events.

___ Yes   ___ No   ___ Uncertain

Now, go back over the survey and place your fiancé's initial in the spaces to show how you think he or she would respond.

3. Your Family of Origin's Influence

When two people marry they bring together two distinct personalities, ways of thinking and acting, expectations about negotiating emotional closeness, and styles of resolving conflict. Many of these factors are a result of our formation by our own families. The task of a newly married couple is to blend and integrate these many factors into a style that they can call their own.

Family researchers have identified certain factors that have formed us as individual family members. One such researcher, R. H. Moos, has identified ten "family factors" that influence our personalities, our personal preferences for solving conflict, and our communication styles.[1] A couple beginning marriage faces the task of blending and integrating these factors. Each factor is presented below, followed by a few reflection questions that will help you identify both your family of origin's style and the personal preferences that you bring into your marriage.

4. Factors Which Form Relationships

In the chart below evaluate whether your family was Low, Medium, or High in each factor by placing your initial followed by a L, M, or H on the first line provided. Leave the second line blank for now.

Emotional Closeness: The extent to which family members express closeness to each other and the degree to which family members are helpful and supportive of each other.

Was your family Low, Medium, or High in "emotional closeness?" _____ _____

Expressiveness: The extent to which family members are encouraged to express their opinions and feelings in an open manner.

Was your family Low, Medium, or High in "expressiveness?" _____ _____

Conflict: The extent to which conflict is dealt with directly. Also, the extent to which family members are allowed to openly express anger.

Was your family Low, Medium, or High in the way it dealt directly with conflict? _____ _____

Independence: The extent to which family members are encouraged to make their own decisions and to solve their own problems.

Was your family Low, Medium, or High in encouraging family members to make decisions and solve their own problems? _____ _____

Achievement: The extent to which the family encourages members to be achievement-oriented and/or competitive regarding school, sports, and careers.

Was your family Low, Medium, or High in encouraging family members to be achievement-oriented or competitive? _____ _____

Intellectual/Cultural: The way the family is concerned about or engaged in wider social, educational, and cultural matters.

Was your family Low, Medium, or High in promoting involvement in wider social, educational and cultural matters? _____ _____

Recreational: The amount of emphasis placed by the family on various kinds of sports and recreational activities.

Was your family Low, Medium, or High in encouraging family members to get involved in sports and other recreational activities? _____ _____

Moral/Religious: The extent to which the family gives priority to religious expression and formation in religious and moral values.

Was your family Low, Medium, or High in placing an emphasis on religious expression and formation in religious and moral values? _____ _____

Organization: The importance placed on things like planning of recreation or family meetings, financial planning and responsibility, clear boundaries and responsibilities within the family.

Was your family Low, Medium, or High in its level of organization, such as the way financial planning was done and the way responsibilities were given? _____
_____

Control: How power and authority are exercised in the family. For instance, were parents clearly in charge; did they exercise authority in a firm, loving manner or rigid, sometimes authoritarian manner?

Was your family Low, Medium, or High in the way authority and discipline were exercised? _____ _____

Go through each factor again, marking your fiancé's initial followed by a L, M, or H in the second space provided to indicate how you think your future spouse responded to each factor.

Reflecting Together

1. Of the ten factors, are there any that you think your own family of origin accomplished in a successful manner? Which ones? Of the factors, which represent your own family of origin's greatest strengths?

2. Many newly married couples decide to do some things differently than the way they were done in their own families of origin. Of the ten factors, are there any that you either want more or less of? Why?

3. Using the ten factors as your starting point, what do you admire most about your future spouse's family of origin? Is there anything you admire about his or her family that is not included in the ten factors? What?

4. Of the ten factors, which ones were accomplished in a similar way by both of your families? Which ones represent a different approach? (For instance, one family might be very expressive and another less expressive.)

5. Blending Your Approaches

We are sometimes taken by surprise by the many small traits, habits, and patterns that our partner brings into marriage that are different than what we expected or what we are used to. For instance, a wife might be taken by surprise that her husband is unexpectedly "messy," not hanging up his clothes when going to bed each night. These unexpected differences range from small things like forgetting to put the toothpaste cap back on, to bigger issues like not being in the habit of balancing one's checkbook.

Marriage is about combining or blending different ways of doing things, attitudes about work and friends, and preferences regarding how time will be spent. The assumption that many engaged couples make is that they know each other quite well, so there won't be many big surprises later. While this may be generally true, we need to keep in mind one big factor that can influence "before marriage" and "after marriage" behavior—the difference between courtship behavior and marriage behavior.

Simply put, courtship behavior tends to be a bit more high-energy and forgiving than does marriage behavior. Common sense tells us this is true. When we are courting we are often caught up not only in the "excitement of the chase," but also with the romance. Because we are so interested in our intended, we spend more time listening to him or her, sometimes overlooking personality quirks that might normally irritate us. No doubt, any of your friends who have been married for at least three years can tell you stories of "before" and "after." While these stories are often humorous, every once in a while someone tells a story about a significant difference that causes real trouble.

The exercises below are meant to help you identify areas in your personal and work life, as well as social interests and patterns, that might require you to blend together to form a common unity.

Take some time to complete the survey on the next page, placing a check in the box that best matches your response to each statement.

As a married person I'll be OK with . . .

My partner having friends of the same sex.

❑ Yes ❑ No ❑ Unsure

My partner having friends of the opposite sex.

❑ Yes ❑ No ❑ Unsure

My partner playing in a weekly sports league.

❑ Yes ❑ No ❑ Unsure

My partner stopping at the bar to talk with old friends before coming home after work.

❑ Yes ❑ No ❑ Unsure

My partner working the same hours that she or he worked before we were married.

❑ Yes ❑ No ❑ Unsure

The amount of time my partner spends on personal interests and/or hobbies.

❑ Yes ❑ No ❑ Unsure

My partner and I taking separate vacations.

❑ Yes ❑ No ❑ Unsure

Reflecting Together

1. Do you know any married couples that have talked about differences in behavior or attitudes "before marriage" and "after marriage"? What differences do you remember them describing?

2. Rank the following items from 1 to 10, with 1 being the most important in building a life together.

___ Communicating desires, dreams, needs

___ Participation in religious activities

___ Respect

___ Willingness to forgive

___ Common value system

___ Sensitivity

___ Financial security

___ Loyalty

___ Honesty and trust

___ Commitment

___ Physical affection

___ Other: please list

6. Marriage as a Journey

How can we describe this journey of marriage? It is a journey of discovery in which we learn about ourselves individually and as a couple. It is a journey of passion and excitement in which we strengthen the bond that unites us. And sometimes it is a journey of sorrow in which we console each other in our losses.

The image of a journey is an intriguing one for marriage. In marriage we often journey together, hand in hand. Sometimes we wander our own roads, however, taken away from our spouses by the path of our work or by our own foibles and failures. When our road takes a different path, we need to stop and reflect. Does this path threaten the framework of our marriage? Should we change it? Sometimes it will be difficult to return to our spouse and walk the same road together again. Yet marriage is a commitment to do just that, as this passage from the Old Testament Book of Ruth beautifully expresses:

> Do not press me to leave you
> or to turn back from following you!
> Where you go, I will go;
> where you lodge, I will lodge;
> your people shall be my people,
> and your God my God.
> Where you die, I will die—
> there I will be buried (Ruth 1:16-17).

Our popular culture seems to have picked up on the journey theme to express what love means between two people. Reflect for a moment on some of these lines from songs that have become part of our cultural identity:

I'm making my way back to you . . .
The long and winding road that leads to your door . . .
Like a bridge over troubled water . . .
You'll never walk alone . . .
He's got a ticket to ride . . .

As we reflect on marriage as a journey that makes God's presence real, we are invited to imagine that God is somehow present in our journey, even when the road is bumpy or actually disappears from our view. The disciples of Jesus once took a journey with him across the Lake of Galilee and became very afraid when the wind and rough waters threatened to swamp their boat. They were frozen with fear, helpless, worried, thinking that they weren't going to make it. But they did. With the help of God, they pulled through.

In the journey of marriage God is the unseen partner who journeys with us. The introduction to this book described a couple who were traveling on the Sunday following the death of Jesus. As they walked, they met a stranger who joined their party. They told the stranger everything about Jesus, not realizing that the stranger was really Jesus. It was only when they "broke bread" together that they realized that the previously unrecognized stranger was in fact Jesus. Your journey as a married couple will be much the same. Like the couple on the road, your participation in the Eucharist together will provide an opportunity to recognize Jesus in your marriage. Sometimes, it is only in retrospect that we recognize God's presence with us.

The theme of journey reminds us of the choices that we make as our lives unfold. Often, we are not aware of the impact of these choices until later in life. The many choices you are making now are important—choices concerning wedding plans, where to live, where to work, how much time to spend with family and friends, and so on. One of the most basic choices present to you as you begin your married life is to "walk by faith and not by fear." Let God be the guiding force in your life and integrity, respect, love, and honesty be the road on which you travel. Such a path may well be the road less traveled, but the choice to take it can, as the poet Robert Frost has written, make "all the difference."

7. Constructing Your Timeline

In the space on the next page construct your own personal timeline. Place your date of birth at the beginning and your wedding date at the end. In between mark significant events, noting their date, your age, and important things that you associate with them—people, places, or cultural markers (e.g., songs, movies, or books). Also note your image of God at the time and your image of God as you approach your wedding date.

Birth   **Wedding Date**

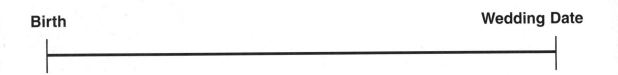

In the space below write a short note to your partner describing the impact that he or she has had on your journey so far. Use the information from the timeline to clarify how your journey progressed before meeting him or her. Address also your hopes and expectations for how the two of you will journey together in your marriage.

Case Study 1

Jim and Mary knew each other for two years before they were engaged. Last year they became
more serious with each other, and they have just
announced their engagement. Mary's parents
live a couple of hours away, and she phones them
every two or three days. Sometimes she talks
with one or both of them for as long as an hour.
At first, Jim thought of Mary's calling as quite
positive; he came from a family where there was
a lot of emotional distance and little physical
show of affection. He thought that Mary's family
had a lot to teach him about closeness. But sometimes her calls have interfered with their plans or
taken away from their time together. Now that
the decision to marry has been made, he is realiz-

ing that he isn't just marrying Mary, but her family as well. What if she continues
to call her parents every two or three days when they are married? Jim has some
fears and jealousy about the time Mary spends talking with her family. The few
times he has attempted to communicate them to her, Mary has become defensive
and indicated that she had a right to talk with her parents. He now has concerns
about who will come first in Mary's life, him or her parents.

Reflecting Together

1. What would you advise Jim to do in the above case study?

2. What do you think is an acceptable pace of visiting your in-laws and your family (once a week, monthly, etc.)?

3. List below any concerns about your future in-laws' involvement with the two of you after you are married.

4. Do you think it will be easy or difficult for your partner to set appropriate limits with his or her parents and to stand up for you when necessary? If not, why not?

Case Study 2

Paula and Dan had known each other for four years before becoming engaged. Their courtship was without serious tension, and their engagement was just as smooth. Both had taken the task of preparing for marriage quite seriously and they were well prepared for marriage. They had sought out the advice of people who had been married for many years in the hopes of anticipating whatever trouble would come their way. What they didn't anticipate was that Paula would get a better paying job than Dan, one that required a good amount of travel. What Dan didn't expect were the feelings of jealousy, depression, and even anger that came over him at odd moments. Their arguing increased, followed by alienation. Dan became more resentful of Paula's being on the road so much, and he became even more dissatisfied with his own work situation.

Then, when driving by the church one day, Dan dropped in to talk to a priest about his situation. The priest made a referral to a marriage therapist where Dan was able to face his fears and his feelings of inadequacy. Both Paula and Dan were able to refocus their own goals and reconnect to their previous feelings of concern and care for one another. The result of this was that Dan began to do some serious career planning and work on his own issues of self-confidence and esteem. Both know that they will still have to settle the issue of care-giving for a new baby (when that time comes), but both are feeling more confident in their ability to discover solutions.

Reflecting Together

1. In the above case how difficult do you imagine it was for both spouses to come to a solution? Do you think it is more difficult for a man or a woman to ask for the kind of help that Dan asked for? Why?

2. Can a situation like the one described above "wreck" a marriage? Why or why not?

3. What four or five things will you commit to doing should your marriage be threatened for whatever reason?

---

1. Moos, R. H. *Combined preliminary manual: Family, Work and Group Environmental Scales*. Palo Alto, CA: Consulting Psychologists Press; 1974. See also, *Family Therapy: An Overview*, Goldenberg & Goldenberg, Brooks/Cole Publishing, Belmont, CA, 1991 (p. 276-77).

3

Establishing Emotional and Sexual Intimacy

In this session you will explore the meaning of intimacy and sexuality and clarify your own criteria for what it means to be in an intimate relationship. As part of this exploration you will reflect on various aspects of love and what you can do to maintain and grow in the intimacy you share. Also, you will reflect on the Church's understanding of sexuality.

1. Faith at the Heart of Your Marriage

Christian marriage is one of the seven sacraments. We speak of sacraments as signs which point to the deeper reality of God and God's kingdom. In Christian marriage we can also say that your marriage points toward a deeper reality working within the two of you. It points to the love that Christ has for the Church, a love that led him to the ultimate sacrifice of his own life. As a sacrament, marriage is an "efficacious" sign of Christ's love of the Church. This means that a sacrament not only points toward a deeper reality, it also builds that very reality. As a sacrament, marriage points toward the love Christ has for the Church while at the same time deepening the love a man and woman have for one another.

The *Catechism of the Catholic Church* states: "On the threshold of his public life Jesus performs his first sign—at his mother's request—during a wedding feast. The church attaches great importance to Jesus' presence at the wedding at Cana. She sees in it the confirmation of the goodness of marriage and the proclamation that thenceforth marriage will be an efficacious sign of Christ's presence" (#1613).

Reflecting Together

1. If your marriage points to anything, what do you want people to see? (Check one or more of the answers that applies to you.)

❑ That love conquers all

❑ The reality of forgiveness

❑ A model for how people can get along

❑ Two people really in love

❑ That love has a service dimension to the world

❑ God's love for all people

❑ That the world can be a better place

❑ Other:

2. Can you think of anyone who has been a sign for you of God's love present in the world? What qualities did you see in this person that you admire?

3. Are there any personal tendencies or patterns that might get in the way of your being a sign of God's love for your spouse?

4. In thinking of family life, what are two or three values or qualities you want your children to experience because of your love for them?

*T*he entire Christian life bears the mark of the spousal love of Christ and the Church. Already Baptism, the entry into the People of God, is a nuptial mystery; it is possible to describe baptism as the bath which precedes the wedding feast, the Eucharist. Christian marriage in its turn becomes an efficacious sign, the sacrament of the covenant of Christ and the Church (Catechism of the Catholic Church, #1623).

2. Emotional Nurturing and Intimacy

In the last one hundred years Western psychology has put forth numerous theories of why people do what they do, theories that pay attention to how our development as children affects the way we enter relationships as adults.

Eric Erickson, in his book *Childhood and Society*, reflects on the meaning of intimacy. He writes:

> Intimacy involves an overlapping of space, a willingness to be influenced and openness to the possibility of change. Only a strong and flexible identity can move toward intimacy. As a young adult I must be able to come close to another person in a way that enables that person to know, to influence, and possibly

to alter the boundaries of myself as I know them. I must accept the risk of being changed, of coming to a different awareness of who I am. If I am unsure of who I am, if my movement through adolescence has left me still confused or deeply defended, then the risk implied in intimacy will seem too great (p. 74, *Childhood and Society*).

Reflecting Together

1. If intimacy involves an "overlapping of space, a willingness to be influenced and openness to the possibility of change," how have you been influenced and changed so far by your relationship with your partner?

2. What signs or signals does your partner give that tell you that he or she is stressed or upset?

3. How would someone know when you are stressed? What is your form of body language that signals to another what is going on?

4. What is the best thing that you can do for your fiancé when he or she needs comfort and nurturance? What is the worst thing?

3. What Is Intimacy?

With the above description of intimacy in mind, take some time to do the exercise below and the questions that follow. What do you need or expect from an intimate and nurturing relationship? (List in order of priority, with "1" being most important.)

____Praise   ____Affection

____Feedback   ____Sharing of Hurt

____Friendship   ____Sharing of Anger

____Challenge   ____Sharing of Interests

____Attention   ____Commitment

____Company   ____Trust

____Time for Solitude   ____Other: (please list)

Place an E for "easy" or D for "difficult" next to each word to indicate whether it is easy or difficult for you to give the following to your partner when he or she is upset or hassled.

____Praise   ____Affection

____Feedback   ____Sharing of Hurt

____Friendship   ____Sharing of Anger

____Challenge   ____Sharing of Interests

____Attention   ____Commitment

____Company   ____Trust

____Time for Solitude   ____Other: (please list)

4. What's Love Got to Do With It?

It comes as no surprise that the word "marriage" is associated with the word "love." The second Vatican Council beautifully described the love of marriage when it stated: " Such love, merging the human with the divine, leads the spouses to a free and mutual gift of themselves, a gift proving itself by gentle affection and deed" (*Gaudium et Spes*, 49). Yet, two people often have different ideas about the meaning of the word "love." Before you begin your marriage it might be helpful to clarify and expand on your notion of love and how its meaning will define your married life.

Listed below are three ways we can talk about love: as a feeling, as a committed stance, and as an unfolding process. Each of these three ways has a distinct contribution to offer a couple. Each has a distinct drawback or pitfall if the couple places too great an emphasis on one aspect to the exclusion of the other two. Take a look at how each is described and complete the reflection section that follows.

LOVE AS	DESCRIPTION	BENEFITS	PITFALLS	EXAMPLE
Feeling . . .	Love experienced primarily as a feeling that impels one person toward the other	Energy and passion become the glue that hold the couple together. Emphasis on spontaneous shows of affection.	When the feeling, energy, or passion fails or dies down, is love over? We fear our spouse saying: "I don't love you, the feeling is gone."	Two people meet, fall passionately in love. Two years later the routine of married love, demanding work schedules, perhaps the first child makes it difficult to recover the original feelings.
Committed Stance . . .	Love experienced as a commitment to a set of values such as loyalty, fidelity. Emphasis on one's duty to maintaining his/her part of the relationship.	Common set of values becomes the glue that holds the relationship together. The couple can be confident of an underlying unchanging foundation.	An over-emphasis on duty can make it difficult to allow the other person to change and develop. We fear our spouse changing because it might threaten our underlying foundation.	A serious life event (death of a parent, job loss, illness) causes one spouse to begin a reexamination of his/her life. The other spouse says, "You're changing, that's not fair!"
Process . . .	Two people see their relationship as a process involving a life-long dialog about how we understand ourselves, how we change and mature over time, and how our lives are linked.	Change and development is allowed provided the couple has worked out a set of rules that govern how they will continue to communicate and resolve differences.	Hidden and/or unclear expectations concerning communication and dialog can lead to confusion, hurt, and anger.	A couple finds that because of work and family schedules, they are spending less and less time with each other. They resolve to find the time to work on their process of love.

Reflecting Together

1. Does it make sense to you that a healthy marriage needs all three types of love: as a feeling, as a committed stance, and as a process of growth and change?

2. Suppose that love was like a mutual fund and that these three aspects of married love were three mutual funds that you could invest in. Make a pie chart from the circle below to show what percentage of your investment you would put into each fund.

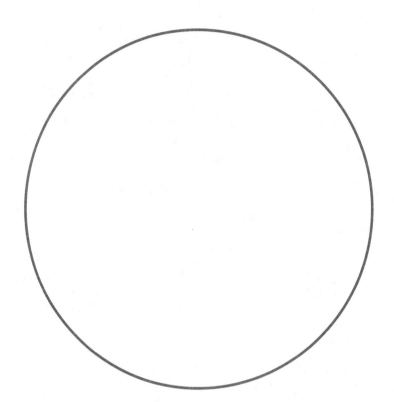

5. Rules for Intimacy

To maintain a marriage over time all three types of love are needed. Perhaps the most overlooked of the three is love as a process of growth and change whereby we continue to create intimacy with one another. We are used to thinking in terms of feelings and commitment when we talk about love, but often forget that our ability to grow and change in the way we express our love over time is equally important.

Listed below are a concrete set of "rules for intimacy" that might govern the way a couple works their "process of love" through the course of their marriage. Take a look at this sample set of rules, then complete the exercise that follows.

Rules for Intimacy

- We will commit to being honest about our thoughts and feelings.

- We will commit to being open to change.

- We will commit to not sharing intimate details of our married life unless we have talked to each other about this.

- We will commit to finding appropriate ways of communicating with each other if our communication becomes strained.

- We will commit to asking for outside help if we reach an impasse.

Check which of the intimacy rules listed below you expect to find difficult at which you expect to find easy.

Easy	Difficult	Unsure	
❏	❏	❏	When we argue we will make up before going to bed.
❏	❏	❏	I will seek out regular and frequent opportunities to communicate with my spouse concerning how my work is going.
❏	❏	❏	If my spouse does or says something hurtful to me, I will bring this to his or her attention as soon as possible without retaliating.
❏	❏	❏	I will not share information about my spouse with others without first asking his or her permission.
❏	❏	❏	I will be open to changing personal habits that cause concern to my spouse.

Easy   Difficult   Unsure

❏   ❏   ❏   If my spouse and I begin drifting apart and we can't turn things around by ourselves, I will agree to seek advice/counseling from a priest or therapist.

❏   ❏   ❏   I will be honest with my partner concerning how I am feeling on any given matter.

❏   ❏   ❏   I will seek my spouse's forgiveness when I am wrong.

What other rules not listed above would you include in your own personal "rules for intimacy?"

6. Exploring Sexual Love

Sex and sexuality are essential aspects of married life. The Church teaches that married life is meant to be fully human, total, faithful, exclusive until death, and "fecund," or fruitful (*On Human Life* #9). Sexuality plays an important role in reaching the goal of becoming fully human. Our view of sex cannot be separated or isolated; it is part of who we are as people with bodies, minds, and spirits. Since the Church's view of sexuality is holistic, it reminds the couple that their own sexual love mirrors the love of God the Creator. Marital love is meant to be fruitful. In his design of marriage, God envisioned a love that would fruitfully expand into a community of familial love. The urge to love fully and completely and to express that love through the procreation of children is part of our God-given nature.

The *Catechism of the Catholic Church* expresses the two ends of married love this way:

> The spouses' union achieves the twofold end of marriage: the good of the spouses themselves and the transmission of life. These two meanings or values of marriage cannot be separated without altering the couple's spiritual life and compromising the goods of marriage and the future of the family. The conjugal love of man and woman thus stands under the twofold obligation of fidelity and fecundity (#2363).

Thus, the two great purposes of Christian marriage expressed through sexual intercourse are the "unitive" and the "procreative" (*On Human Life* #12). And while we can separate the two ends in the abstract in order to understand their meanings, we cannot really separate them in practice. In a sense, the Church is saying that the unitive and procreative are two dimensions of married love. Thus, every act of married sexual love calls for an openness to children (*Humanae Vitae*, Par. 9).

The United States Catholic Bishops, in reflecting on responsible conscience formation in the areas of sexuality and child-bearing, wrote:

> First of all, the Church teaches that it is the couple alone, following their morally responsible conscience judgments, who are to decide those many "when" and "how" issues (*Faithful To Each Other Forever*, p. 40).

The following represent the criteria laid down by the Bishops concerning a well formed conscience (p. 40). After each there are one or two questions that a couple might ask in forming their conscience on this matter.

Openness to life. Do I accept the Church's teaching that the very nature of conjugal love requires that it be open to life? Do I see children as the greatest possible and most precious gift of marriage?

Generous and sacrificing, not selfish. Are our decisions on family planning motivated merely by a desire to have more time, money, or possessions?

Trusting. Am I willing to take the risks involved in bringing a child into the world, not being motivated by fear, but trusting that with God all things are possible?

Wise. Have we taken into account all the factors involved in a decision to have a child, including our own mental and emotional readiness?

Humble. Do we recognize that fundamentally God is the source of all life, and that even in an unplanned pregnancy we can see the unfolding plan and mystery of God's presence?

Mutual. Do we recognize that the decision to have children is not just about a biological process, but one that needs to take into account our whole selves, including our deepest spiritual impulses?

Church-guided. Do we look to the Church not as one teacher among many, but as an authoritative, Spirit-guided, and essential source of formation for our conscience? Are we willing to consult the necessary authority (often a parish priest or pastoral minister) when we are in doubt or confused concerning the question of family planning?

Next, take some time to complete the short survey below. This will help you articulate your attitudes and expectations about sex and sexuality and how you wish to integrate them in your marriage. Check the appropriate box for each statement.

Agree	Disagree	Unsure	
❏	❏	❏	Emotional contact with my spouse is essential to a fulfilled sex life.
❏	❏	❏	Sexual intercourse is just another form of communication. The way the marriage goes, so goes the couple's sex life.
❏	❏	❏	In order to be fun, sex should be spontaneous.
❏	❏	❏	I want my partner to tell me if something I am doing during intercourse is either not helpful or hurtful.

Agree Disagree Unsure

❑	❑	❑	I want to spend time with my spouse caressing and holding each other before we make love.
❑	❑	❑	It's OK if lovemaking is used to relieve tension.
❑	❑	❑	I can and will respect my spouse's wants and needs, especially if he or she doesn't want to make love on a given day or night.
❑	❑	❑	The two ends of marriage are the good of the spouses and the transmission of life.
❑	❑	❑	If children should come early in our marriage, I am ready.
❑	❑	❑	In addition to expressing my love for my spouse, I expect our sexual life to be fun and passionate.
❑	❑	❑	It will be easy for me to talk with my spouse regarding what gives me pleasure.
❑	❑	❑	I won't be able to make love with my spouse if we are arguing and feuding.

Reflecting Together

1. How did your parents view sexuality? How did they express their sexuality in their relationship when you were growing up? For instance, were they open or private about physical affection with one another?

2. What messages were you given by your parents concerning sex and sexuality? Is there anything you would change about how your parents taught and modeled sexuality to you?

Consider Natural Family Planning

Natural Family Planning (NFP) refers to a set of practices and methods employed by the husband and wife to either avoid pregnancy or to assist in becoming pregnant. Because the methods employed do not interfere with the woman's naturally occurring cycle, and because they do not rule out the possibility of the transmission of life, Natural Family Planning, when used with the proper intention, preserves the nature of sexual intercourse as the Creator established it. For these reasons, the Church approves NFP.

NFP is based on scientific research into the process of ovulation that occurs in pubescent women. Approximately every month the ovaries of a woman release an egg, which then begins its journey down the fallopian tubes. As this occurs the woman's cervical mucus begins to increase and become more slippery and stretchy. The purpose of this watery mucus is to protect, nourish, and assist the sperm in the event that intercourse occurs during the fertile period. If fertilized, the ovum attaches itself to the walls of the uterus and a pregnancy is now under way. If not fertilized—and the window for fertilization is only about four to five days—the body of the woman begins to prepare for another egg to be released by a slow but steady rise in temperature. As the temperature rises, the rich lining of the uterus is shed through the process of menstruation. As the woman's temperature rises, she experiences a drying of her vaginal mucus.

Once a husband and wife become educated together about the woman's cycle of fertility they begin to understand that there are two indicators of fertility—dropping temperature and increasing slippery and stretchy mucus, and two indicators of infertility—rising temperature and the drying up and disappearance of cervical mucus. Both of these indicators, when combined together, are known as the sympto-thermal method because it requires checking for both the temperature and cervical mucus. The ovulation method only checks cervical mucus of the woman.

Research has shown that Natural Family Planning has a 99.6% effectiveness as a method for preventing pregnancy.[1] The method does place some discipline on the man and woman. Both are asked to attend a training session so that they can understand in fuller detail not only the physiology of the woman's cycle but how the method is administered. Training sessions teach both the man and woman how to observe temperature and vaginal mucus and how to chart the changes throughout the time of the cycle. As such, NFP requires some attention to the details of the woman's cycle.

The discipline involved in the method is offset by the significant gains that the husband and wife often attain when they employ this method. Both are required to participate together in understanding the cycle of fertility and both develop a greater awareness of each other's bodies.

Also enhanced is the communication between the two; because they work together they often feel a deeper unity of purpose. And because the method is natural and holistic, the couple often reports a more relaxed manner of sexual intercourse.

What is often overlooked by couples is the fact that NFP is an excellent method to use when a couple experiences difficulty in getting pregnant. A couple almost never expects to experience difficulty getting pregnant and when this happens it can be quite unsettling. Doctors often recommend that the couple attend NFP workshops as the first response to difficulties in getting pregnant. Using this method, a couple will be able to maximize the possibility of fertilization.

7. Taking Responsibility for Married Love

The following are specific ways that married couples take responsibility for their sexuality and the expression of that sexuality in the art of lovemaking. After each point you will be asked give your reaction.

Make the bedroom a safe and sacred space. When one considers the intimacy of sexual intercourse it becomes clear that both the husband and wife need to feel relaxed and safe if they are to give deeply of themselves. This means that the bedroom needs to be a place of relaxation.

• Don't make the bedroom a place to resolve arguments; make it a place to make up and reconcile. Decide what room(s) are the places you will resolve conflict.

• Don't make the bedroom a place for work; if possible place your computer station in a den or another room. Some people feel that even a TV in the bedroom distracts the couple from attending to their needs.

❏ I want to think about this some more ❏ Doing OK with this for now

Comments for myself or my fiancé:

Feel comfortable with our bodies. In our fashion-conscious society it may come as a surprise that not all of us are completely comfortable with our bodies. We may feel too short, overweight, clumsy, or just plain. Our body images affect the way we enter into lovemaking. Part of lovemaking means communicating all of this to our spouse and giving empathy, understanding, and encouragement. Daily stress also takes its wear and tear on our bodies as well as our spirits. All of this affects our sexual response. It is always advisable to talk about this with our spouse if this is an issue.

❏ I want to think about this some more ❏ Doing OK with this for now

Comments for myself or my fiancé:

Realize that our sexual responses are sometimes different. This seems like a "no-brainer," yet this truth is often the cause of great deal of tension between spouses. This ranges from expectations of how many times per week a married couple will have sex to how sexual relations are initiated. Some people can suspend the day's worries and make love to their spouse; others need to talk about the day's worries before they make love. Not checking these differences out with the other person can lead to hurt feelings and anger.

❏ I want to think about this some more ❏ Doing OK with this for now

Comments for myself or my fiancé:

Don't use pornographic materials as part of your lovemaking. With the advent of the VCR and cable TV, the ability to view pornographic material has become much easier. Pornography detaches sexual intercourse not only from the context of marriage but also from its human meaning as well. Further, the couple themselves introduce a voyeuristic pattern that has unhealthy and harmful implications for their relationship if it becomes a pattern. Consider too that the great majority of X-rated films take the perspective of the male. In them, women are clearly objects of pleasure for the man.

❑ I want to think about this some more   ❑ Doing OK with this for now

Comments for myself or my fiancé:

The story is told of a young married couple who were given a "sex manual" as a wedding present. To the couple's surprise the parents of the groom asked to see the manual. After about a two-week period they handed the book back to them and said, "This doesn't leave much to the imagination. We preferred to find out for ourselves."

Reflecting Together

1. Do you think there is any wisdom in the reaction of the parents of the newly married couple?

2. What is your expectation concerning how the two of you will educate yourselves concerning your own sexuality and sexual responses?

8. Marriage as a Conversation

In the book of Genesis we discover that before the first sin both Adam and Eve were on intimate terms with God. Apparently, God was used to taking evening strolls through the garden and conversing with Adam and Eve. We know this because on the first early evening after they had sinned they hid themselves when God decided to walk in the coolness of the evening.

Imagine being on such friendly terms with God that we could converse as if we were intimate friends! We should all enjoy such a relationship with God. Our tradition has taught us that conversation with God represents the core of our relationship. We speak of prayer as conversation with God and we can talk of our scriptures as being the record of the ongoing conversation between God and God's people. We even speak of Jesus as the Word of God, the final self-communication of God as love born into our world.

Consider for a moment that the sacrament of marriage begins with a conversation between two people through the taking of marriage vows. Actually, the conversation that is marriage probably begins on the first day we meet our future spouse. And while we have countless conversations with our partners over the years, there are three major characteristics of how marriage can be framed as a conversation. They are:

- Marriage as a conversation between best friends

- Marriage as an honest conversation

- Marriage as a conversation involving God

Marriage as a Conversation Between Best Friends

Married people often speak of their spouses as their best friends. Many of us have the expectation that the person to whom we are married will be our best friend. Yet, if this is so we need to express in more realistic terms what we are willing to do to maintain the friendship and where we can improve. Check the response that best expresses where you are.

Sharing of intimate knowledge about yourself

 ❑ Can do better   ❑ Doing OK

Keeping of confidentiality

 ❑ Can do better   ❑ Doing OK

Seeking advice from each other

 ❑ Can do better   ❑ Doing OK

Encouraging your spouse to develop emotionally, spiritually, and physically

❏ Can do better   ❏ Doing OK

Taking time to develop your friendship with your spouse

❏ Can do better   ❏ Doing OK

Marriage as an Honest Conversation

If nothing else, we expect that we will be able to speak honestly with our spouse. But this can be difficult, since we also want safety and acceptance from our spouse. Being honest doesn't mean being cruel, but it does mean opening up to our partner—and being open to hear from him or her—in the tough times as well as in the easy.

Striving to be open and vulnerable with one's partner

❏ Can do better   ❏ Doing OK

Openness to partner raising difficult questions

❏ Can do better   ❏ Doing OK

Openness to partner intervening if you are doing something harmful to yourself or your relationship

❏ Can do better   ❏ Doing OK

Commitment to exploring fears, hopes, and expectations for your relationship

❏ Can do better   ❏ Doing OK

Marriage as a Conversation Involving God

Sometimes we give lip service to the importance of spirituality and don't take our relationship with God seriously until a personal crisis or momentous decision is facing us. Admitting that a greater power than ourselves is at work in our lives helps us keep perspective; it helps us remember that our lives are a loan to us from God, and that we will not live forever.

Understanding that personal prayer deepens the marital relationship

❏ Can do better   ❏ Doing OK

Taking time for personal prayer, even if it is five minutes a day

❏ Can do better   ❏ Doing OK

Fostering a realization that there is a higher power in your life

❏ Can do better   ❏ Doing OK

Resolving differences in religious preferences and practices

❑ Can do better ❑ Doing OK

Taking time to pray as a couple

❑ Can do better ❑ Doing OK

Taking time to identify rituals and prayer patterns that foster your relationship

❑ Can do better ❑ Doing OK

Reflecting Together

1. What common rituals or practices (going out to eat, the family picnic) did your family of origin have?

2. What daily or weekly practices or rituals can the two of you do together to enhance the quality of your marriage (daily prayer, meals, weekly church attendance, etc.)?

3. How do you imagine prayer and participation in the sacraments can enhance the total life of a marriage?

4. Are there one or two couples that you admire for the honesty they seem to have in their marriage? Who are they and what characteristics do they embody?

Case Study 1

Lisa and John have been married for two years. Both are working professionals. Lisa works as an accountant for a large corporation. In the past few months she has received a promotion and has been placed under increasing pressure to learn her new duties. She prides herself on doing a job well and is hard on herself when she feels she isn't performing up to her own standards. Throughout their marriage Lisa and John have consistently shared how the day has gone and the positives and negatives about their jobs. Lately Lisa has begun to be more critical of her superiors and her coworkers. Every so often she just "blows up" and vents her anger toward "people who don't do their jobs, leaving me  to pick up the pieces." Just two days ago she had a particularly tough day where her immediate supervisor put pressure on her to complete a task more quickly. That day she was particularly angry. John has allowed her to vent her anger and has tried to patiently offer suggestions to her. He has been getting more frustrated because his suggestions seem to go nowhere with Lisa. Today things had gotten much worse. Lisa was again very angry at her work. John suggested to Lisa that she try to talk to someone at work about all the pressures she is under, only to have Lisa blow up at him and shout, "Why do you always take their side? I don't need to be told what to do. I'll just solve things myself." This was the first time that Lisa's anger had been directed toward John. He felt hurt and attacked by Lisa, and withdrew emotionally from her.

Reflecting Together

1. In the above example what do you think each person needs in order to get back to a sense of intimacy and togetherness?

2. Would you agree that when we are under stress it is more difficult to maintain an open, communicative relationship with those we love? If yes, why do you think this is so?

3. What would you do in a situation similar to the above? Have you ever had to work toward repairing trust in a relationship so that you could continue enjoying a high level of intimacy? What did you do to repair the trust?

Case Study 2

J. and D. have been married for four years. They both work and have one child, age two. When they were first married they made love three to four times a week, sometimes more. Since the birth of their son the frequency of lovemaking has been reduced to once or twice a week. They have both discussed the lack of time to talk, let alone to make love. Both J. and D. strive to stay in touch with the other and respect each other's need for rest and relaxation. Lately,

however, D. has had difficulty with the decreased frequency of lovemaking. D's feelings have been that of frustration, and frankly, D. is also feeling increased sexual energy and attraction toward J. When D. has mentioned this J. has felt defensive and guilty. If only J. would feel the same toward D. Both J. and D. swore that they would not blame each other when sexual needs weren't met (both of their parents had tension concerning this issue). Now they are facing a real problem. D. feels the lack of sexual contact, and J. feels inadequate and guilty.

Reflecting Together

1. In the above case study, who do you think is the man? Who is the woman? Why?

2. Do you think the above represents a realistic scenario for the normal tensions that occur in a couple's sexual life? What suggestions would you give to this couple to resolve their problem?

3. Do you think there are differences between the way a man experiences his sexuality and the way a woman does? How do you characterize these differences?

1. *Faithful to Each Other Forever*, Bishop's Committee for Pastoral Research and Practices, Washington, D.C., 1988.

4

A New Family Circle

In this session you will have an opportunity to reflect and dialog on your expectations, hopes, and fears about becoming a parent. You will also have an opportunity to examine how you were parented as a child and how becoming a parent will stretch the circle of intimacy so that the needs of a newborn are attended to. This is not always an easy task. There are, in a sense, two children to be cared for: the newborn infant and the still new relationship that exists between you and your spouse.

1. Faith at the Heart of Your Marriage

Planning a wedding brings us face-to-face with the fact that there are more than two people involved in a marriage. It's not simply you and your fiancé planning your wedding; you are planning an event that brings together a network of families, relatives, and friends. In a sense, it's their wedding too! Preparing for a wedding reminds us that we belong to a community. In addition to the communities just mentioned, we belong to a faith community. Marriage is a celebration of community, among family, friends, and the Church.

Community is not only a part of your wedding day; it will be part of your life together in the future. We believe so much in this sense of community that the Church has even described marriage and family life as the "domestic Church." This concept implies that the Church exists at the very basic level of family life. In a way, marriage and family life represent the basic community not only of the Church, but of the larger culture. The community of marriage and family reminds us that we exist not as solitary individuals, but as participants in a wider community. Being a "domestic Church" challenges us to create a distinctively Christian home in which the Catholic faith is consciously practiced.

As a community, family members have an unbreakable bond. As a priest once said in a homily on family life: "You can fire an employee at work, but you can't fire a family member; your relationship with that member may be strained, but you can't ever fully deny that you are connected to each other." The sacrament of marriage calls us to look at our family relationships in this way. At the same time, marriage often provides the grace we need to love unconditionally.

This unconditional love is a mark of your relationship as a couple as well as your future relationship with your children. It is by this love that you best communicate your faith to each other and your children. As the Second Vatican Council said: "Christian married couples help one another to attain holiness in their married life and in the rearing of their children. . . . In what might be regarded as the domestic Church, parents are the first heralds of faith with regard to their children" (*Dogmatic Constitution on the Church*, #11).

Reflecting Together

1. What do you think of the idea that family life is one of the basic building blocks of the Church and the wider culture, and that a Catholic Christian family strives toward the total unconditional acceptance of every member of the family?

    ❑ Sounds right to me.

    ❑ The "unconditional acceptance" part is awesome.

    ❑ The "unconditional acceptance" part sounds right, but might be hard to achieve.

    ❑ I have to think more about this.

2. The call to marriage implies that Christian marriage somehow makes the world a better place. If someone asked you how your marriage will make the world better, what would you say?

3. When you think of making a "community of two" with your fiancé, what place does the role of personal and shared prayer play in making this community happen? Have the two of you discussed the possibility of having some shared prayer together and your future participation in the Church's worship?

4. The Church teaches that parents are the first teachers of their children. What do you want to teach your children about God and the Church? About the world?

In the Latin Church, it is ordinarily understood that the spouses, as ministers of Christ's grace, mutually confer upon each other the sacrament of matrimony by expressing their consent before the Church (Catechism of the Catholic Church, #1623).

2. How Were You Parented?

The reality of parenting doesn't really hit us until we become parents ourselves. Even for a couple seriously preparing for marriage, the day that they become parents can seem quite far off. And, until the first child comes along, it is difficult to say with certainty just what type of parents we will be. We just have to wait until we get there.

On the other hand, we already know something about the type of parent we will be because we have been to parenting school for at least eighteen years. When push comes to shove and we are pressed to know what to do with our own children, we usually turn first to what we were taught and modeled by our own parents. So it makes sense to get in touch with your own experiences of how you were parented.

The first step in understanding how your family experience has shaped your attitudes and beliefs about being a parent is to understand how you felt about your family position. Basically, we can categorize family position by stating that there are three possible experiences: that of being an oldest, middle, or youngest child in the family. All of us ultimately answer for ourselves whether we liked being the oldest, middle, or youngest child in our families. Each position has its benefits and drawbacks.

3. Your Family Position

Take some time in the exercise below to identify your family position and circle any description that comes close to describing your experience as either a oldest, middle, or youngest child. Note: "Only" children often experience a mix of oldest and youngest characteristics. If you are an only child select the characteristics that best match your experience growing up.

Oldest Child

Is often the recipient of high expectations from his or her parents.

My experience: Yes   No

Can sometimes feel that he or she doesn't live up to parental expectations.

My experience: Yes   No

Middle Child

Can feel frustration over his or her contributions to the family going unnoticed or unrecognized.

My experience: Yes   No

Might become competitive with older sibling(s).

My experience: Yes   No

Youngest Child

Can be considered "spoiled" by older siblings.

My experience: Yes   No

May become used to older siblings taking initiative and may have to fight to be heard.

My experience: Yes   No

Oldest Child	Middle Child	Youngest Child
Can be seen as the "third parent" and be asked to assume baby-sitting and looking after of younger siblings.	May begin to feel "lost," especially if he or she doesn't have a trait or talent that helps define a position in the family.	Can feel more secure and loved by parents.
My experience: Yes No	*My experience: Yes No*	*My experience: Yes No*
Sometimes the oldest girl in a large family feels taken advantage of, especially if she is asked to do more household chores than her older brother.	Is often open to new experiences and doing things in a new way.	Often has the freedom to develop more creative expression (art and music).
My experience: Yes No	*My experience: Yes No*	*My experience: Yes No*
May have a difficult time letting go and having fun.	Sometimes defines self in contrast with older sibling: if older sibling is cooperative and compliant, the middle child may be more oppositional and combative.	Sometimes develops a defensive posture of not sharing information with other family members because he or she feels parents and older siblings will be too critical.
My experience: Yes No		
Position of the eldest is often envied by younger siblings.		
My experience: Yes No	*My experience: Yes No*	*My experience: Yes No*
The oldest is often the "trailblazer" for younger siblings in that he or she forces parents do deal with new parenting issues.	Can sometimes feel compared to an older or younger sibling.	Is able to sit back and watch the interaction of older siblings with their parents.
My experience: Yes No	*My experience: Yes No*	*My experience: Yes No*
May resent the fact that parents were easier on younger siblings than they were on him or her.	May resent the authority given to an older sibling by his or her parents.	May feel "left behind" by older siblings and seek to "catch up" by either excelling at school or by acting out.
My experience: Yes No	*My experience: Yes No*	*My experience: Yes No*

Other: (please describe any other experiences)

Reflecting Together

1. How does your family position affect the way you interact with your partner?

2. How does your partner's family position affect the way he or she interacts with you?

4. Parenting Styles in Your Family of Origin

Take some time to identify how your parents defined their role as parents and how they exercised their authority in your family. By doing this you can get in touch with what you consider the positives and negatives about your own family situation. This will also help you think about which traits you want to foster in your own parenting and which you want to change.

What style of parenting did your mother and father exhibit as they raised you? Place an "M" next to the following roles that your mother assumed and a "F" for the roles that your father assumed in the way they parented you.

_____captain of the ship   _____a benevolent dictator

_____a friend   _____an educator

_____conductor of an orchestra   _____chairperson of the board

_____a drill sergeant   _____other images:

_____a coach

Using what you identified in the above exercise, place a check next to the parenting style that best describes your parents' way of parenting.

___ **Authoritarian**

Parent has total control. There are clearly defined, almost rigid, limits and children are punished, often severely, for stepping outside these limits. Children are seldom allowed to challenge parents. Anger and fear are used to control children, and children know they belong by conforming to the wishes of the parent. Rules can appear arbitrary and made up at the whim of the parent. Feelings are often suppressed and/or ridiculed. Love can seem conditional: "If you love me, then you will behave this way or do this thing. . . ."

___ **Permissive**

In this family there are few limits, and children often have a lot of freedom. Children may know they are loved by the parent, but may not thrive because of the chaos present by too few limits and rules. A child in this type of family might be forced to assume parental responsibility because one or both parents are not present either physically or emotionally.

___ **Validating**

There are clearly defined limits and rules, but children know they are loved and cared for. Instead of punishment a child learns that there are clear and consistent consequences for his or her behavior. Rules are enforced consistently, and children are allowed to express their feelings and receive validation for them. High support and high structure characterize this type of family.

Reflecting Together

1. Some people who do this exercise state that their experience was actually a blend of two of the three styles listed above. If this is true for you, which of the styles were blended in your family?

5. Your Parents' Disciplinary Techniques

It is no surprise that the role of a parent is to provide authority and structure. There are various ways of maintaining order in the family, with varying consequences on the self-image of the developing child. Take some time to assess what techniques your parents used to maintain order. Place a checkmark next to the techniques that were used in your family of origin.

____ Punishment

This form of discipline consists of either physically spanking the child or depriving him or her of something that he or she desires. Punishment requires a parent to be resolute in following through when an ultimatum is served. Spanking a young child might get his or her attention, but has the potentially negative effect of either hurting the child or escalating into more serious forms of hitting.

____ Reward

This form of discipline consists of giving the child something that he or she wants for a desired behavior. The "gift" can be a physical thing, like a toy, or a relationship thing, like time spent with Mom and Dad. It usually is based on a loose sort of contract between the child and the parent that goes something like this: "The more responsibility you show, the more reward (to be defined) you will be given."

____ Shame

This is a kind of discipline where the child is ridiculed openly and frequently, often in front of others. There is usually a good deal of anger associated with shaming someone. It has great potential to damage a child because the child often cannot escape the humiliation and put-downs of an angry parent. Shame produces a great deal of internal anger that can later come out when the child becomes big enough to physically express it.

____ Logical Consequences

This form of discipline arises from clearly defined set of consequences for specific undesirable behaviors. A child knows in advance the consequence for misbehavior. This approach is beneficial in that it detaches a parent's anger from the discipline.

____ Natural Consequences

This form of discipline places the parent in the position of allowing the child to accept responsibility for the natural consequences of his or her actions. For instance, the natural consequence for leaving one's baseball mitt outside in the rain is that it is ruined. The parent, in this example, holds firm that the child has to accept responsibility for this by either paying for a new one or going without one.

Reflecting Together

1. What were the dominant forms of control and discipline in your own family of origin? How do you want to discipline differently? Which of the forms of discipline listed above do you think you and your partner will employ?

2. Were there any harmful behaviors that your parents engaged in that you told yourself you would never repeat with your own children (for instance, abuse of alcohol, abusive relationship, domestic violence)? Can you speak about them in this session, or do you prefer to speak privately to your fiancé about them?

6. Becoming a Parent

Becoming a parent is perhaps the most significant transition that a married couple experiences. For as much as we prepare for being a parent, there is nothing like the reality of the transition to remind us that things have changed. While the transition can be an exciting time, there can also be a mixture of fear and anxiety mixed in with the excitement.

The good news about all of this is that research indicates that couples who have relatively intact communication and feedback systems tend to be able to weather the changes that occur in parenthood without too much of a negative effect on the marriage. But it pays to be prepared for the transition and to develop strategies that enable a couple to continue to communicate about their hopes, fears, anxieties, and even disappointments that center around parenthood.

Listed on the following page are just a few transitions that will occur in becoming new parents. Go through them and check off your immediate reaction to each of them.

	Excites me	Scares me	I'll let my spouse do it	I won't like it but I'll do it
For women: Watching your body change throughout the pregnancy	❑	❑	❑	❑
For men: Watching your spouse change throughout the pregnancy	❑	❑	❑	❑
For women: Morning sickness	❑	❑	❑	❑
Anticipating what our baby looks like	❑	❑	❑	❑
Deciding on names for our baby	❑	❑	❑	❑
Getting the baby's room in shape	❑	❑	❑	❑
For women: Taking care of myself during pregnancy	❑	❑	❑	❑
Going to childbirth classes	❑	❑	❑	❑
Going into labor	❑	❑	❑	❑
Bringing our newborn home	❑	❑	❑	❑
Changing diapers	❑	❑	❑	❑
Doing baby's laundry	❑	❑	❑	❑
Getting up with baby during night feedings	❑	❑	❑	❑
Taking baby to the doctor	❑	❑	❑	❑
Staying up with a sick baby	❑	❑	❑	❑
Taking time off from work to be with baby	❑	❑	❑	❑

Reflecting Together

1. What hopes do you have for your future child(ren)?

2. What fears or concerns do you have regarding the world into which they will be born?

7. Marriage as a Growing Garden

One of the more important images that comes to us from the Bible is that of a garden. For Christians, the garden represents the idyllic time when we enjoyed complete unity with God. The Book of Genesis begins with the story of creation, and the image of a garden is central:

> Then the Lord God planted a garden in Eden, in the east, and he placed there the man whom he had formed. Out of the ground the Lord God made various trees grow that were delightful to look at and good for food, with the tree of life in the middle of the garden and the tree of knowledge of good and bad (Gen 2:8-9).

Of course, we know that our first parents, through their own choice, forfeited their place in the garden. They were banished from it as a consequence of their sin. As a result, all kinds of evil would enter the world: brother would be pitted against brother, husbands and wives would have conflict, childbearing would be painful, humans would have to work long and hard to just make it in the world. The list could go on and on.

Turning to the New Testament we can find hints at a restoration of our original innocence in the Gospel of John. Here, we read that Mary of Magdala went to the tomb of Jesus on the third day only to find Jesus' body missing from the tomb.

> (Mary) turned around and saw Jesus there, but did not know it was Jesus. Jesus said to her, "Woman, why are you weeping? Whom are you looking for?" She thought it was the gardener and said to him, "Sir, if you carried him away, tell me where you laid him, and I will take him." Jesus said to her, "Mary!" She turned and said to him, in Hebrew, "Rabbouni" which means teacher (Jn 20:14-16).

It is in Jesus that our lives are restored. If our lives are like gardens where we are asked to cultivate good works, love our spouses, and care for our children, then Jesus is the Master Gardener who makes all things grow.

Suppose your marriage is like a garden, where God asks you to produce good works, love each other, and bring into the world and care for children. Play with this image in your mind for a moment. As anyone who works in a garden knows, there is ground to prepare, weeds to clear, and seeds to plant. Then, when the plants emerge, there is a need for constant care.

The most important thing needed for any garden is water. Without water plants will wither and die. Water is the life source of your garden.

Think of the spiritual life source of marriage as love and respect. As water is to a garden, love and respect is to a marriage. Without them a marriage, like a garden deprived of water, will gradually wither and die. And as we know, God is the True Source of all love and respect.

Reflecting Together

1. Using the image of marriage as a garden, suppose you had a well in the midst of the garden, with the water being composed of love and respect. Can you think of anything that could either poison the water of love and respect or cause the well to go dry?

2. Water is the life source of all gardens. The Church makes use of water in the sacrament of baptism. What were you taught about what baptism does to a person? Why or why not would you baptize your child?

3. Is there any way your parish can help you make the transition into parenting when that time comes?

4. What religious practices can you and your fiancé observe that will help you face the inevitable changes that will occur in your future and thus keep the life source of love and respect alive?

5. How will the choices you are making now about lifestyle or career influence how you think about children and their upbringing?

Case Study 1

Dan and Judy have been married for eight years and have two children, a boy (eight) and a girl (five). They had been talking about a third child and felt that the timing was right; both had jobs they enjoyed and they were able to save for another child, knowing that Judy would want to take some time off after their child was born. But suddenly their world had been turned upside down. Judy had been diagnosed with cervical cancer. This had been followed by a quick succession of events: surgery, involving a complete hysterectomy, followed by chemotherapy.

Both had the sense that their faith allowed them to weather these tough times. Judy emerged from treatment cancer-free and her prognosis was good. She went through a period where she felt empty and robbed of the opportunity to bear another child. However, through various support groups she was able to come to grips with the reality of her situation. Dan was very supportive throughout the course of the crisis. He surprised himself, however, by having more of a difficult time with the fact that Judy would not be able to conceive a child. About six months after the surgery and with Judy's recovery going successfully, he began to suggest the possibility of adopting another child. To his surprise Judy was not open to the suggestion; she felt that since her cancer had required a hysterectomy her days of rearing a newborn were over. In the few weeks after bringing up the topic of adoption Dan found himself alternating between edginess and sadness. A friend of his suggested that he might be mildly depressed as a result of the finality of the situation. Further, he suggested talking to someone about how Dan was reacting to Judy's not wanting to consider adoption.

Reflecting Together

1. A crisis like the one above can put a tremendous strain on a marriage. What do you think has to happen in order for the above marriage to become stronger?

2. Are there ways that a religious perspective can help in the above case? Are there ways that a religious perspective can be harmful? Explain.

3. What do you think of Dan's response of wanting to consider adoption? Is there any "right" answer in this case? What would you advise this couple to do in order to address any possible tension as a result of Dan and Judy being on different sides of the issue?

Case Study 2

Charlie and Angelica were married two years before their first child was born. They were blessed with a healthy baby boy. At the time of their son's birth they were full of energy for the task of becoming new parents: they attended childbirth classes together and read about all the developmental changes that took place not only within the womb but also during the first 18 months of life. They both had agreed that after their son was born Angelica would quit her full time job with the phone company to provide full-time child care. They were financially well off and they both felt comfortable with that decision. Angelica suffered some post-partum depression but managed the transition adequately. She became involved in a mother's day out program and also volunteered in a number of programs. All in all they had made the transition to being new parents rather well.

Then, slowly, things began to change. Charlie got a promotion that took them to a new city and away from both of their parents. Their son was now two years old. Angelica faced the task of finding new friends and making new social contacts. Charlie was gone more as his job demands increased. And Angelica began to have more "blue" periods in her life; she missed her parents' support and the friends she left behind. And now that her son was more mobile and was ready to go to day care she began to plan to work part-time. Both she and Charlie agreed that she was too isolated and that part-time work would be a good solution.

Today, Angelica and Charlie faced a significant but unexpected reality. Angelica is pregnant! Here was news that took both by surprise. Angelica knew immediately that she had to place her own plans on hold. She also felt more fear now that she was miles away from her own parents and network of friends. For his part Charlie was stunned. His own work schedule would increase, not diminish, over the next ten months. He and Angelica had already argued about his work schedule. He was worried that the tension would only increase. Both were silent for a time as they let the reality sink in. Both wanted to be happy and positive about this news, but they knew they would have to do a lot of talking and working through their feelings about their new situation.

Reflecting Together

1. Do you think it is "unchristian" or selfish for Charlie and Angelica to have such a reaction to this unexpected pregnancy? Why or why not?

2. What do you think each has to do in order to make their situation into a positive choice for life instead of seeing the pregnancy as an intrusion? What is required of Charlie? Of Angelica?

3. In the case above do you see any signs of potential trouble for this couple that could later, if not addressed, lead to serious marriage difficulty? What are they?

4. How do you think you and your fiancé will react if something similar should happen to you?

5. What would you want from your future spouse in facing such a challenge?

5

Dealing With Conflict

In this session you will explore your own style of conflict resolution and your preference for dealing with conflict when it occurs. You will also have an opportunity to learn about four ways of handling conflict that can seriously harm a marriage. Finally, you will learn a method of resolving conflict that relies on communicating effectively as the first response to any conflict.

1. Faith at the Heart of Your Marriage

As we've already discussed, every marriage has more than two parts to it. There is you, your partner, and a third reality—the relationship you create. There is a synergy in marriage where the totality of a marriage is truly more than the sum of the individual parts. The love of husband and wife expresses itself in ways that the spouses could never have dreamed of, creating a deep union.

From the perspective of our faith, we can say that this threefold dimension of a marriage is a reflection of the Trinity. The Trinity is perhaps one of the deepest mysteries of our Christian tradition. Our Creed speaks of "One God, three persons" to express the unique nature of God. Though this is a great mystery, one thing is certain: the Trinity speaks to the reality that God exists in a community of love. Marriage participates in the life of the Trinity by God's grace and in seeking to imitate the community of love which is God.

To say that the Trinity is a community of love is to say that there is an unfolding dialog between Father, Son, and Spirit. So, too, marriage is meant to be an unfolding dialog of love between husband and wife, a dialog characterized by respect and unconditional regard for the other.

Of course, we all know that the love of God is a perfect love and that the way we love is flawed and imperfect. We sometimes fail to meet our ideal of loving deeply and experience both internal conflict and conflict with our spouse. The *Catechism of the Catholic Church* states: "Every man experiences evil around him and within himself. This experience makes itself felt in the relationships between man and woman. Their union has always been threatened by discord, a spirit of domination, infidelity, jealousy, and conflicts that can escalate into hatred and separation" (#1606). This brings us face to face with the need to engage in conflict resolution and reconciliation, so that our love for one another can be perfected throughout the life of our marriage.

Reflecting Together

1. React to the thought that marriage participates in the life of the Trinity by the creation of community and an unfolding dialog of respect and unconditional regard for the other.

❑ Wow! I have to think about this.

❑ I don't get it.

❑ The thought that I find God in our love for each other sounds right.

2. Personal sinfulness affects the way we enter into relationships. The *Catechism* lists discord, jealousy, a spirit of domination, infidelity, and other conflicts as examples of how sin can threaten a relationship. How has your own experience of sinfulness affected your relationship with each other?

3. The sacrament of reconciliation provides an opportunity to experience God's forgiveness and to receive the grace we need to deepen our marital union. Have you considered celebrating this sacrament as part of your preparation for marriage?

4. Do you know of anyone who is a model to you of going beyond conflict to reconciliation where a "win/win" situation is created? What have you learned from this person concerning resolving conflict?

5. Our love is imperfect and often requires us to ask forgiveness of the other. Is this something easy or difficult for you to do? Is forgiving easy or difficult?

It can seem difficult, even impossible, to bind oneself for life to another human being. This makes it all the more important to proclaim the good news that God loves us with a definitive and irrevocable love, that married couples share in this love, that it supports and sustains them and that by their own faithfulness they can be witnesses to God's faithful love (Catechism of the Catholic Church, #1648).

Our Response to Conflict

When interviewing for a job as an office manager a prospective candidate for the job was asked how she felt about conflict between office workers. She responded emphatically: "I hate conflict!" Her response to the question could easily sum up many people's response to conflict. We simply don't like dealing with conflictual situations.

Perhaps the main reason we dislike conflictual situations so much is that we know that conflict often creates a "win-lose" situation. One person wins, and the other loses: feelings can be hurt, and power can be used to "put people in their place." Even if we think we are the ones who will "win," it can be uncomfortable. It's difficult to tell a friend or loved one something truthful that may cause hurt feelings.

It is especially important to think carefully about conflict in our closest relationships. In these relationships we are able to speak more freely, which can create greater intimacy and personal growth. On the other hand, when we have such a high degree of familiarity, it can be easier to speak in ways that are disrespectful or demeaning.

3. Getting in Touch With Your Conflict Style

Take some time to respond to the following statements and questions. They are designed to assist you in understanding your and your fiancé's approach to conflict.

When there is conflict between us, my fiancé's first tendency is to (check those that apply):

❑ avoid the whole issue

❑ become quiet and withdrawn

❑ become angry

❑ become aggressive

❑ try to soothe things

❑ overcriticize

❑ respond with humor

❑ become defensive

❑ give advice

❑ get cynical

❑ respond with sarcasm

❑ blame me or others

❑ raise his or her voice or yell

❑ try to listen

❑ Other: (please describe)

When there is conflict between us my first tendency is to (check those that apply):

❑ avoid the whole issue   ❑ overcriticize   ❑ respond with sarcasm

❑ become quiet and with-drawn   ❑ respond with humor   ❑ blame myself

❑ become defensive   ❑ raise my voice or yell

❑ become angry

❑ give advice   ❑ try to listen

❑ become aggressive

❑ get cynical   ❑ Other: (please describe)

❑ try to soothe things

Reflecting Together

1. What aspects of your partner's way of handling conflict do you find helpful? In other words, what does he or she do or say that helps in the resolution of conflict?

2. Is there anything about your partner's way of handling conflict that you do not find helpful in resolving conflict between the two of you?

3. Describe how your own parents resolved conflict in your family. Utilize the checklist provided above.

4. What positive messages and behaviors did you learn from your parents about dealing with disagreements and conflict?

4. Conflict Resolution Begins With Clear Communication

Effective conflict resolution is really just a form of good, clear communication where we utilize strong "I" statements and strive to define the problem that focuses on specific behaviors. When any significant event occurs in our lives (be it happy or sad) we usually want to talk about it with those who are close to us. Our response to any event has two parts: a feeling-reaction, as well as a belief or way of thinking about the event. All of this influences the way we act or behave toward the person or persons involved in the original event. The following chart outlines a pattern of how we respond.

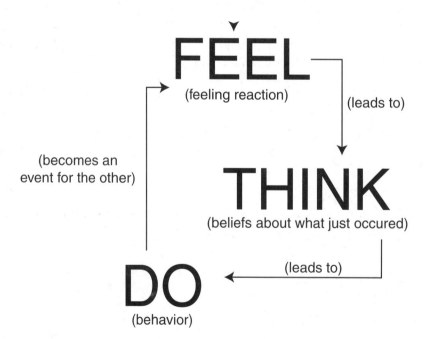

EVENT LEADS TO

FEEL
(feeling reaction)

(leads to)

THINK
(beliefs about what just occured)

(leads to)

DO
(behavior)

(becomes an event for the other)

Suppose a husband (who is happily married) becomes intensely involved in a work project and forgets to inform his spouse that he will be late for a dinner engagement. As a result he is an hour late. This is the event. The feeling-reaction of the wife is most probably one of worry, anger, and hurt. This is because she is sitting at a restaurant not understanding why he is not there. She may even believe or think that he has been involved in an accident, or that he simply doesn't care. As a result she may act in a way that shows her spouse anger, hurt, and displeasure. Her behavior then becomes an event for the other spouse.

Understanding How Communication Happens

We often underestimate the complexity involved in communicating and listening to another. Many fights get started not because people want to fight but because they react to what the other says instead of really listening.

Look at the diagram below, which describes what happens when a person, the sender, attempts to communicate with another, the receiver.

Dynamics of Communication

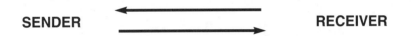

SENDER   **RECEIVER**

1. Every communication involves two people, the SENDER and the RECEIVER. Even before the SENDER begins to speak, he or she is influenced by:

> **Beliefs** about how the world works and how people act;
> **Attitudes** toward the future and his or her expectations for an outcome;
> **Generalizations** and **assumptions** about people's behaviors and their motives;
> **Stereotypes**: rigid generalizations attached to a specific group of people.

2. The message between the SENDER and the RECEIVER is not only the words spoken. The SENDER encodes the message and then the RECEIVER decodes it.

3. How does the SENDER encode the meaning?

> **Verbal:** The listener picks up on only 7% of a message communicated through verbal content;
> **Voice Tone:** 38% of the message that the listener hears is communicated through voice tone;
> **Body Posture:** 55% of what the listener hears is communicated through body posture.

4. How does the RECEIVER decode the meaning?

> **Feelings:** As sender talks, the receiver has an immediate feeling-reaction about what he or she is hearing;
>
> **Thoughts:** As sender talks, the receiver has immediate thoughts and beliefs about what is being said;

Actions: The receiver has a tendency to react through the use of a behavior (sigh, dirty look, rolling of eyes) to the sender's message, especially if the atmosphere is charged.

5. The Feel, Think, and Do pattern operates in both the SENDER and the RECEIVER.

SENDER becomes a RECEIVER often before he or she is finished sending, and then goes through his or her own "think, feel, do" cycle. The communication of the sender becomes the event that triggers the cycle.

RECEIVER quickly becomes a SENDER. We talk at a rate of 100-120 words per minute (wpm). Our internal dialog (our self-talk) moves at around 600 wpm. This explains the tendency to not only "mind-read" the other, but to interrupt as well.

Reflecting Together

1. Does it surprise you that we have a tendency to pick up more from tone of voice and body posture than from words when another person communicates with us?

2. What do you believe is the biggest block for you in listening to your fiancé?

5. Legitimate/Reasonable Requests of the Other

The above cycle of event, feelings, beliefs (about the event), and behavior can become a vicious circle where spouses continually react to each other's behavior without the benefit of seeking and giving feedback to the other. Good communication will allow a couple to focus on specific behaviors that are significant to the detriment or development of their marriage.

Look at how someone might communicate feelings and thinking to his or her spouse while making a valid request for negative behavior to change or positive behavior to continue. The first example is taken from the incident described above. The second example is a communication about something positive. This way of communicating works equally well with both the negative and positive events that occur in any relationship.

Person Communicating Feelings and Thoughts

EVENT
(Describe the
event, focusing
on the behaviors
of persons involved.)

Example One: *When you didn't call to let me know you'd be late . . .*

Example Two: *When you brought me flowers yesterday . . .*

**FEELING-
REACTION**
(Describe how
you felt.)

Example One: *I felt . . . angry . . . sad . . . irritated . . . hurt. . .*

Example Two: *I felt . . . happy . . . excited . . . surprised . . .*

**DESCRIBE THE
CONSEQUENCE**

Example One: *Because I had to eat alone after preparing a meal for the two of us.*

Example Two: *And it really made my day.*

**THOUGHTS/
BELIEFS**
(Describe what
you are thinking
about the behavior.)

Example One: *I thought maybe you didn't respect me since you didn't call.*

Example Two: *It really shows that you care for me.*

WHAT YOU WANT

Example One: *I want you to agree to be more considerate the next time. Does that seem reasonable to you?*

Example Two: *You can send me flowers any time you want, and who knows, maybe I'll surprise you one of these days.*

6. Good Communication Takes Practice

Take some time to think of a positive event that happened this past week that involved both you and your fiancé in which your fiancé played an active role. First, describe the event in the "event" column. Next, construct a description of the event, placing emphasis on your fiancé's action. Then, describe how you felt, what you were thinking about the event, and what you want to see happen in the future.

EVENT	EVENT DESCRIPTION	FEELING REACTION	THOUGHTS/ BELIEF	WHAT YOU WANT
Write a brief description of the event.	*Construct a statement describing your fiancé's action in the event.*	*Let your fiancé know how you felt.*	*What were your hidden thoughts about the event?*	*What would you like to see happen in the future?*
	When you . . .	I felt . . .	I thought to myself *or* was thinking . . .	And I want you to . . .

7. Knowing How to Fight Fairly

Listed below is a step-by-step strategy to minimize the harmful effect of unresolved conflict. Take some time to review the procedure before practicing this with your fiancé.

Conflict Rules

- Treat the other with respect by the use of eye contact, calm voice tone, non-threatening body posture, and respectful speech.

- Listen to the other until you understand the other side. Good listening involves being able to restate the other's content, meaning, and feelings in such a way that he or she signals "you got it."

- Communicate respect for the person. Make sure that the focus is on a specific behavior, feeling, or value. It is important to signal the other that the issue is not about his or her person, but about a specific behavior or statement.

1. Begin with content summary: "Tell me what happened . . ." or "Tell me what is making you so angry. . . ."

2. Move to content validation: "You're saying that. . . ." Keep this going until the other indicates that you have heard the content correctly.

3. Move on to feeling validation: "You seem angry about this. Is that so?" or "You're feeling left out of the discussion and as a result you feel. . . ."

4. Don't forget meaning validation: "I can see that being included means a lot to you. . . ."

- Only after you have gone through content, feeling, and meaning validation do you move on to state your position and feelings on the matter.

- Sometimes it is important to agree to disagree. This can only happen if both parties agree to treat the other with respect.

- Once a person is feeling listened to and the tension is decreased, move on to problem-solving. If possible, ask the other if he or she has thought of any solutions. Offer yours as well.

Now, practice with your partner the main steps of conflict summary, conflict validation, feeling validation, and meaning validation. The best way to practice is to think of a recent conflict and then take turns being the listener and validator of content, feelings, and meaning. Use the exercise above on communicating feelings, thoughts, and beliefs about an event. Remember, the listener needs to work on the four-step process of summarizing content, validating content, validating feeling, and validating meaning before giving his or her response to the issue.

8. Conflict Checklist

Listed below are statements about conflict that are taken from "people in the know" who have commented on conflict. Place a checkmark next to those statements with which you agree, then add any other insights that you have come across that can teach us about resolving conflict.

Seek first to understand rather than to be understood. Stephen Covey (*Seven Habits of Highly Effective People*) maintains that giving the gift of understanding is the beginning of personal effectiveness and conflict resolution.

❑ Agree ❑ Disagree ❑ Easy for me to do when I'm relaxed

❑ Difficult to do when I'm stressed ❑ Doing OK with this for now

Comments:

Don't put off until tomorrow the conflict that can be solved today. Another way of saying this is, "Don't go to bed angry." Healthy marriages benefit from the timely resolution of problems. Making avoidance a habit will begin to harm the relationship.

❑ Agree ❑ Disagree ❑ Easy for me to do when I'm relaxed

❑ Difficult to do when I'm stressed ❑ Doing OK with this for now

Comments:

For every finger pointed in criticism there are three that point back towards you. Think of the times when you have literally or figuratively pointed your finger at someone. Three of your fingers point the other way, towards you. This is another way of saying that when I criticize I may be refusing to recognize my part in the creation of a problem.

❑ Agree ❑ Disagree ❑ I tend to do this when I'm stressed

❑ Doing OK with this for now

Comments:

In any problem between you and me there exists two parts to the problem, yours and mine. Murray Bowen, one of the founders of the Family Therapy Movement maintained that in a relationship problem each person had to figure out what part of the problem was his or hers and take responsibility for it. Speaking first about your part of the problem signals the other that you are not trying to blame and criticize.

❑ Agree   ❑ Disagree   ❑ Easy for me to do when I'm relaxed

❑ Difficult to do when I'm stressed   ❑ Doing OK with this for now

Comments:

Blaming and criticizing are just different ways of avoiding responsibility for a problem. According to John Gottmann, family therapist and researcher and author of *Why Marriages Fail or Succeed*, these are "below the belt" ways of fighting. When we engage in any of them, the argument is prolonged and we often feel that the other is not respecting us.

❑ Agree   ❑ Disagree   ❑ Not a problem when I'm relaxed

❑ Difficult to do when I'm stressed   ❑ Doing OK with this for now

Comments:

Hurt that is not dealt with eventually turns into anger. When someone we love does something that is hurtful to us we often have a "window of opportunity" to share our hurt. If, for some reason, our hurt is not acknowledged it is likely that we will become angry. Dealing with hurt requires two sorts of action: to talk to the other when I'm hurt and to listen to the other when he or she is hurt.

❑ Agree   ❑ Disagree   ❑ This has happened to me before

❑ I'm good at talking to my fiancé when I'm hurt

❑ I'm good at listening when he or she is hurt

Comments:

Each person who enters into a relationship brings a unique style of communicating and dealing with conflict. Marriage represents a blending of these styles. It comes as a surprise to many married people that their "best friend" often has a different way of responding to anger and conflict.

❑ This is true for the two of us   ❑ This is not true for the two of us

❑ My fiancé's style of conflict resolution sometimes drives me crazy

Comments:

Couples can make their marriage a safe place for resolving conflict by agreeing not to use sarcasm or put-downs. This piece of wisdom goes without saying; yet, how easily we forget when we are tired and under stress.

❑ Agree   ❑ Disagree   ❑ Not a problem in our relationship

❑ Sometimes a problem in our relationship

Comments:

While it happens frequently, it is not a good idea to keep a "list of hurts and gripes" and bring them up to the other whenever you fight. It's difficult to let go of past hurts and grudges against the other person and it's too easy to let these surface as "ammunition" when you're fighting. It's best to solve one problem at a time.

❏ Agree   ❏ Disagree   ❏ Not present in our relationship

❏ Present in our relationship at times

Comments:

Explosive rage and/or physical abuse are signs of serious difficulties and require a commitment to enter counseling. This is another way of saying that there are inappropriate and harmful ways to express anger. The wisdom of the scriptures tells us that our bodies are "temples of the Holy Spirit." We disrespect our bodies when we allow rage, anger, and violence to control our responses.

❏ Agree   ❏ Disagree   ❏ Not present in our relationship

❏ Present in our relationship at times

Comments:

Alcohol and conflict don't mix. It is never a good idea to drink when having a fight with your spouse. Further, a person who drinks frequently runs the risk of lowering his or her control over anger. That is why there is a high correlation between drinking and physical abuse.

❏ Agree   ❏ Disagree   ❏ Not present in our relationship

❏ Present in our relationship at times

Comments:

9. Marriage as Friendship

> . . . A friend is like the bars of a castle.
>
> . . . A true friend is more loyal than a brother (Prv 18:19, 24).
>
> This is my commandment: love one another as I love you. No one has greater love than this, to lay down one's life for one's friends. You are my friends if you do what I command you. I no longer call you slaves, because a slave does not know what his master is doing. I have called you friends, because I have told you everything I have heard from my Father. . . . This I command you: love one another (Jn 15:12-17).

For Jesus, a true friend is one who is willing to sacrifice his or her life for the sake of others. Being in service of others in the community appears to be the highest Christian ideal. But there is much more going on in the above passage. Jesus seems to be suggesting that God seeks to have with us the closeness suggested by the word "friend."

Marriage can be described as a "community of two friends." Consider: in a marriage two people sleep together, share emotional and sexual intimacy, confide in each other, perhaps keep secrets together, and often work on common projects together. Simply put, it is hard to resist becoming friends with each other in a marriage.

On the other hand, when the marriage bond is strained the two married "friends" can feel completely apart and distant from each other. This is why someone can feel lonely in a marriage. There may be times when you feel alienated and cut off from the person you chose to be vulnerable with. Ideally, reconciliation renews the bond of friendship and takes it to a new level. The friendship of mature marriage requires a lot of work, but it has a huge payoff in terms of deepening satisfaction and fulfillment.

What Do You Expect From a Good Friend?

Listed below are a few characteristics that make a good friend. Place a checkmark next to those that match your own criteria for friendship and then add any others that occur to you.

❏ Someone who will listen non-judgmentally

❏ A good sense of humor

❏ Ability to accept me the way I am

❏ Loyalty

❏ Someone who will "walk in my shoes" or "go the extra mile with me"

Others:

The Mystical Component of Married Friendship

The friendship of marriage is unlike any other friendship because married love intentionally collapses boundaries. Simply put, in marriage a couple becomes both physically and symbolically naked with each other. In the course of a marriage each spouse will get to know the other in a way no one else will. This is true vulnerability and is also the reason why a marriage that fails causes so much pain to those involved. Knowledge of a person can be used against the other; married couples know instinctively that intimate knowledge can be used to deaden and kill the trust. Yet, many married couples take the risk to love deeply, to be vulnerable because of the promise of a deeper union that transcends the sum of the individual husband and wife.

There is a synergy of sorts that occurs in a marriage; one and one add up to something greater than just two people. We might call it the mystical unity of God's presence with a married couple. Certainly, there is something greater going on than just the actions of two people; there is a deeper presence felt. This marital synergy points to the same action of the Spirit in creating community out of a gathering of individuals who come together on Sunday to celebrate Eucharist. It is the action of God taking our humanity and stretching us to a deeper unity.

The Choice of Vulnerability

To be a friend to one's spouse implies the choice to be vulnerable, for one cannot love without taking the risk of vulnerability. C. S. Lewis, in his book *The Four Loves*, writes:

> To love at all is to be vulnerable. Love anything, and your heart will certainly be wrung and possibly be broken. If you want to make sure of keeping it intact, you must give your heart to no one, not even to an animal. Wrap it carefully round with hobbies and little luxuries; avoid all entanglements; lock it up safe in the casket or coffin of your selfishness. But in that casket—safe, dark, motionless, airless—it will change. It will not be broken; it will become unbreakable, impenetrable, irredeemable. (p. 169, *The Four Loves*, Harcourt Brace Jovanovich, New York, 1960)

There is paradox in being vulnerable that reminds us of Christ's statements: in order to find one's life, one must lose it; in order to grow, the seed must first die to self; he who seeks to be first must be last. The risk of married love is that our hearts may be broken or hurt deeply. Yet Jesus, the supreme model of love, reminds us that out of this risk can come new life, if only we commit to work at the process of love.

The Risk of Love That I Take With You

In the space below write a short letter to your future spouse that addresses what you willingly risk in order to live a life with him or her. Speak to how you imagine your marriage will stretch you and how you imagine you will grow deeper as a result of the continuing process of love and reconciliation that your marriage will embody. Is this a risk worth taking? If so, tell your future spouse.

Case Study 1

John and Debbie have been married for five years, with one child, age two. Debbie came from a family that was relatively intact; her parents experienced tension and would do a good deal of yelling when they argued, but they always managed to hang in there and work things out. John, on the other hand, came from a "broken" family: his own dad left the family when he was five and he was often placed in the care of his grandparents while his mom went to work. His own relationship with his grandparents was conflictual, in part due to the tendency of his grandfather to discipline him physically and to ridicule and put him down. Both John and Debbie saw in each other a refuge from the yelling that occurred in their own family backgrounds.

Recently Debbie has become more concerned about a recurring pattern in the way they deal with conflict. When they argue John sometimes reaches a "point of no return" when his own yelling appears out of control. Sometimes he throws things, not at Debbie, but at the walls. He had told her that he would never hit or harm her. In their last argument John grabbed Debbie's arms and shoved her against the wall. When the fight was over Debbie noticed that she had bruises on her arms. Just this morning Debbie paid a visit to her parish priest who told her that she had a right to be safe, that she should leave the house if she feared their arguing would turn violent. Additionally, he urged both of them to get into counseling. She was confused because she felt committed to the relationship while at the same time fearful for her safety.

Reflecting Together

1. If the above happened to two of your married friends what would you advise them?

2. Would it come as a surprise to you that about 80% of domestic abuse occurs after the consumption of alcohol?

3. In the above case, did it surprise you that Debbie's parish priest would advise her to leave the house if she feared violence? Do you think counseling can really help a couple such as the one above?

Case Study 2

Bill and Rebecca have been married now for nearly twenty-one years. They have three children ages eighteen, fifteen and eleven. Just recently the two of them decided to get into marriage counseling. There were a variety of reasons for this decision: as their children grew older Rebecca began to feel more restless; the more she tried to talk to Bill about this the more he seemed to avoid her. Also, as the years went by Bill had become more

sedentary in the evenings and his TV watching had slowly but steadily increased. So did his consumption of beer. Rebecca wondered to herself if her husband was developing a problem. Again, whenever she would approach him about this he became defensive. For the last year or so there had been an uneasy truce between the two. Both developed their own interests and attended to them, interacting with each other when it came to attending to their children's needs.

It finally came to a head one day when Rebecca realized that her first child would soon be off to college. She began to ask herself if she wanted to live the rest of her life just "going through the motions." One night she told Bill, "I don't know if I want to stay married if we aren't going to communicate and if we avoid doing things together." This statement shook both of them up and they both felt frightened and threatened. But this eventually led to the two of them seeking marriage counseling to get their marriage back on track. At first, the sessions were rocky as they sought to re-establish trust and to reconnect with each other. They gradually began to get in touch with the energy they felt for each other when they first met and they began to tackle what their marriage would look like once the kids started going to college. As the sessions progressed they noticed significant changes: Bill decided to quit drinking altogether and both of them were spending more time together.

1. Can you imagine a future scenario such as the one above for the two of you? What do you think led to the couple becoming distant from each other?

2. If your spouse ever began to drink more and it was a concern for you what would you do?

6

Facing Change and Keeping Your Foundation Intact

In this session you will reflect on change and how to stay in touch with each other through the years despite all the varied forces that can buffet a marriage and threaten its foundation. By doing some initial reflection now, you will be able to outline certain rituals and behaviors that you and your spouse can adopt to insure that you not only keep in touch with each other, but deepen your relationship as well.

1. Faith at the Heart of Your Marriage

Marriage participates in the call of Christ to prepare for and build God's kingdom. Embracing the call of marriage is to some degree a call to embrace the Church's mission to announce the good news of Christ and his kingdom. Another way of saying this is that married couples are called to make the world a better place, not only for their children, but because they have an inner vision that speaks to the fact that the world can be transformed into a better place.

In the sixties some young people thought it better not to have children because of the tremendous problems facing the world. We know today that this is not the right solution to these problems. Rather, by embracing not only the problems, but our part in creating the solutions, a couple can participate in the greater reality of God's grace working in the world. This occurs, certainly, in the procreating and raising of children, but it also occurs in our commitment to work for economic justice, a less polluted environment, quality institutions of education and work, and many more.

Catholic Christian couples don't hide safely in the confines of their homes, their doors closed off to the world; rather, they become involved with the expectation that with the grace of God the world will become a better place. "Incorporated into the Church by Baptism, the faithful . . . are, as true witnesses of Christ, more strictly obliged to spread the faith by word and deed" (*Dogmatic Constitution on the Church*, #11).

Reflecting Together

1. The following are areas in which I see myself becoming involved in order to help build a better world.

❑ Helping out at the local homeless shelter

❑ Volunteering in a youth program

❑ Volunteering as a Big Brother/Sister

❑ Getting involved with my parish

❑ Working on environmental concerns

❑ Becoming involved in politics

Other:

2. Of the above areas, are there any in which you and your fiancé could be involved together?

3. Research has demonstrated that a common set of religious values will strengthen a marriage. Place a D next to the following items that you are doing already and a W next to those items that you want to consider doing.

___ Weekly attendance at church

___ Personal prayer/scripture reading

___ Joint prayer

___ Regular discussion of social issues

___ Couple's retreat at least once a year

___ Spiritual reading

___ Getting more educated on church teaching on social issues and spirituality

The fruitfulness of conjugal love extends to the fruits of the moral, spiritual, and supernatural life that parents hand on to their children by education. Parents are the principal and first educators of their children (Catechism of the Catholic Church #1653).

2. Change Happens

Even though we live in a fast-paced world with change all around us, our human psychology cries out for stability and structure. While change is inevitable, our reaction to it is shaped by our past experiences and whether those experiences are positive or negative.

Get in touch with your own experience of change. In the space below reflect on and write down one experience where something in your life changed for the positive and another experience where something changed for the negative.

An Experience for the Positive

An Experience for the Negative

Next, react to the following statements concerning change, marking yes, no, or unsure.

Change . . .	Yes	No	Unsure
Is something I'm quite used to dealing with	❏	❏	❏
Is easier to deal with in small doses	❏	❏	❏
Will make our marriage more exciting	❏	❏	❏
Is neither positive or negative; it just is	❏	❏	❏
Is something that happens; it's the way you cope that counts	❏	❏	❏
Can threaten any relationship if the change is too great	❏	❏	❏
Can lead to maturity and a deeper spirituality	❏	❏	❏

3. Something Lost . . . Something Gained

A wise person once remarked that for every significant change that we undergo, whether it is physical, emotional or spiritual, there is always something lost and something gained. This is another way of saying that change costs something. As Jesus reminded us, for a seed to change into a seedling, it must give up being a seed.

We know instinctively that if we live long enough, change will occur around us and in us. As we grow older, there are significant changes in our bodies: we might gain or lose weight, we might lose our hair, we might become better at a skill. Whatever the change, if it has a significant impact on us, we can be assured that something has been left behind if there is to be a potential change for the better.

Take a look at the list below of a few changes that are a normal part of living. With each loss there is a potential gain. After you have gone through the list go back to your experience of both positive and negative change and see if there is a similar pattern of loss and gain. Warning: it may be difficult to find a potential gain if the change you have listed is traumatic and has just recently occurred. Sometimes we struggle to find the potential gain for years and we need to realize that with some tragic changes (for example, the murder of a relative) there is no gain experienced.

CHANGE	LOSS	POTENTIAL GAIN
1. Getting engaged or married	One gives up the excitement (or agony) of being unattached, of possibly "playing the field"	One gains the comfort of being oriented in another's love
2. Move to new city	Giving up of the familiar haunts, moving away from close friendships	Development of new relationships, possibly new independence relying on inner strength to make it
3. Death of close relative or friend	Loss of relationship, loss of presence; perhaps a loss of security	Remembering of relative or friend in a way that gives meaning to one's life; not always easy to accomplish
4. An affair	Loss of trust; an experience that something has died in the relationship	Possible re-choosing of marital values and true reconciliation; reconstruction of foundations of relationship
5. Job loss	Loss of esteem and confidence; fear of not being able to regain lost prestige	Toughening of the "inner-self" by hanging in there with the many job interviews and rejections before landing another job
6. Birth of a first baby	Loss of freedom to sleep in, do whatever you want on a Saturday morning after a long week; loss of the sense of the couple forming the primary "we" of the web of relationships	Moving beyond the sense of being a couple to the sense of being a family; excitement at giving love and taking responsibility for the next generation

7. Physical injury	Loss of a sense of athleticness, sense of movement; contraction of one's boundaries to the four walls of the sick room	Winning through to a new understanding of identity due to facing one's vunerability; confronting the fear of death in some cases

4. Are You Stressed Out?

Planning your wedding and beginning a marriage can be stressful, as you well know. Stress can be a factor not just at the beginning of a marriage, but at any time. Recognizing stress is the first step in dealing with it. Go through the following checklist and check off any of the events that have happened to you in the past six months.

STRESSOR CHECKLIST					
	Job Loss		Death of Family Member		Marital Separation
	New Home		Job Difficulties		Pregnancy
	Graduation From or Starting School		Victim of Crime		Death of Friend
	Marriage or Engagement		Legal Difficulties		Change in Residence
	Divorce		Financial Strain		Problem Pregnancy
	Personal Injury, Illness		Illness of Family Member		Change in Job Duties, or New Job
	Job Promotion		Relationship Difficulties		Other:

If you have experienced four or more of the above stressors, there is a good like-lihood that you may be having some of the following physical symptoms (check any that you are experiencing):

❑ Headaches

❑ Muscle tension

❑ Irritability or increase in anger

❑ Loss of concentration

❑ Anxiety

❑ Feelings of depression and avoidance

❑ Stomach problems (irritable bowel, etc.)

❑ An increase in colds or sinus infections

❑ Difficulty sleeping

❑ Heart racing

❑ Increased drinking

❑ Other: (list any other symptoms you may be experiencing)

We know that there is a correlation between being stressed and our physical health and well being. This is because stress taxes our ability to cope. Think of your ability to cope with stress in terms of a bank account. Any time you experience a stressor that is "out of the ordinary" you make a withdrawal from your "coping" account. If you continue to experience stressors like this, you quickly empty your account and then have to make a loan. Headaches, stomach difficulties, and the like are our bodies' way of telling us that we are going to our "coping" accounts too often without replenishing our funds.

Stress creates in us the well-known "flight or fight" response. We usually have two choices when faced with an unpleasant stressor: we can remove ourselves from the stressor or we can fight it the best we can. Unfortunately, many of us often feel trapped in highly stressful situations with few options.

Relationships are usually the first "victims" of high stress levels. This is because we tend to see our married lives as safe territory where we can unburden ourselves. Unfortunately, instead of unburdening we often "unload" on the other by becoming grouchy, irritable, or perhaps by abusing alcohol, caffeine or other drugs.

The good news in all of this is that we can put money back in our "coping" accounts by doing things that relieve our stress and recharge our energies. There is good stress, called "eustress" that we often inflict upon ourselves to help us recharge and renew. Jogging, riding the latest roller coaster, and rock climbing are just a few ways that people place themselves under eustress. Then there are more relaxing, enjoyable activities that we can do for ourselves that relieve tension: walking by the river, attending a movie or play, visiting with relatives or friends. It's up to us to define the stress-relieving activities that we can do for ourselves.

5. Caring for Yourself and Your Relationship

Change is inevitable in any relationship. How we react to and cope with changes, especially stressful ones, is in our control. Asking how we care for ourselves and our relationship is the beginning of a process of adapting to change.

Listed below are various ways that you might take care of yourselves and your relationship. Place a check next to the ones that are realistic for you to do on a routine basis in order to relieve stress and to continue to build yourself and your relationship. Below each item write how many times a week you need to do this in order to feel renewed.

❑ Reading a good book   Times per week:____

❑ Jogging or other exercise   Times per week:____

❑ Going for a walk   Times per week:____

❑ Getting together with friends   Times per week:____

❑ Praying, meditating   Times per week:____

❑ Talking with spouse   Times per week:____

❑ Pursuing hobbies   Times per week:____

❑ Talking on the phone   Times per week:____

❑ Pursuing an education   Times per week:____

❑ Other: List below other activities that re-charge you and how many times per week you need to do these activities

Unhealthy Ways of Relieving Stress

While it may seem like a contradiction, we often engage in behaviors that temporarily relieve stress but in the long run are not all that helpful. These are behaviors that we regret doing after we have engaged in them. Try to identify your own pattern and any behaviors that you recognize as perhaps unhealthy ways of relieving stress.

❑ Drinking too much   ❑ Overeating

❑ "Dumping" on friends   ❑ Consistently not getting enough sleep

❑ Consistently overcommitting   ❑ Excessive shopping

❑ Ignoring significant relationships   ❑ Shutting down

❑ Blowing up, becoming angry   ❑ Blaming, attacking others

List below any other unhealthy behaviors you engage in when under stress.

6. Developing Rituals of Intimacy and Re-creation

We tend to be creatures of habit and ritual. Many people, for instance, look forward to their first cup of coffee and the morning paper. Rituals are repeatable behaviors that employ symbolic objects and that put us in touch with something meaningful in our lives. For example, many people enjoy barbecuing during the summer after a long day's work. Firing up the grill, drinking a beer, relaxing with family and friends are all part of this summertime ritual.

When a couple gets serious with one another, they also adopt rituals of intimacy and proximity. They might re-visit a favorite park or restaurant to remind themselves of the beginning of their relationship. Rituals also help us to renew our relationship and recall the energies that brought us together in the first place.

Listed below are some common rituals that the two of you might adopt to continually renew your relationship and to tap the original energies of your love for one another. Check the ones that might apply and list others that you already have invented.

❑ Eating meals together   ❑ Going out on the weekends

❑ Planning a mini-vacation   ❑ Praying together

❑ Taking the time to talk and   ❑ Attending church together
cuddle before and after making love

❑ Writing letters or poems to each other

❑ Other: List below the common rituals that you are already doing or want to do that have the potential to bring you closer together.

7. Holiness Is Wholeness

More than forty years ago Fr. Joseph Goldbrunner wrote a book entitled *Holiness Is Wholeness*. This phrase sums up the idea that the quest for holiness is an holistic endeavor involving all parts of the human person: the thinking, feeling, physical, psychological, and sexual parts of who we are, as well as how we were formed in our own families of origin.

In our Catholic tradition we speak of the "Holy Family" of Mary, Joseph, and Jesus. Many people today might not feel particularly "holy," yet all of us are on a quest for "wholeness," for integration that leads to happiness. In the mystery of God, the Holy Family somehow tells us something about what it means to be holistic about integrating all the various parts of our lives. As married people we are asked to become intentional about seeking this integration and placing the Spirit of God in the middle of our efforts.

An important aspect of the quest toward integration, toward holiness, is how we deal with the unsettling aspects of life. This raises the question of suffering, pain, and the disorientation that comes when things go wrong in our lives. Mary and Joseph had to deal with this when they lost Jesus and later found him in the Temple. We read that Mary and Joseph had "great anxiety" (Lk 2:48) over Jesus' absence. And at the end of Jesus' life Mary had to face the greatest fear of every parent: the death of her own son.

It is normal to worry and be concerned about our future. The world is sometimes a tough and threatening place in which to begin a new community of love. Yet the words of Jesus challenge us to take stock of our fears and anxieties. They remind us about the true foundation of anyone seeking holiness and wholeness in our world.

> Therefore I tell you, do not worry about your life, what you will eat or drink, or about your body, what you will wear. Is not life more than food and the body more than clothing? Look at the birds in the sky; they do not sow or reap, they gather nothing into barns, yet your heavenly Father feeds them. Are not you more important than they? Can any of you, by worrying, add a single moment to your life span? Why are you anxious about clothes? Learn from the way the wild flowers grow. They do not work or spin. But I tell you that not even Solomon in all his splendor was clothed like one of them. If God so clothes the grass of the field, which grows today and is thrown in the oven tomorrow, will God not much more provide for you, O you of little faith? So do not worry and say, "What are we to eat? Or what are we to drink? Or what are we to wear?" All these things the pagans seek. Your heavenly Father knows that you need them all. But seek first the kingdom of God and God's righteousness and all these things will be given you besides. Do not worry about tomorrow; tomorrow will take care of itself. Sufficient for a day is its own evil (Mt 7:25-34).

Reflecting Together

1. Do you think Jesus is against planning for the future? How do you interpret this saying: "Do not worry about your life, what you will eat or drink?"

2. Check the statements that correspond to your belief about misfortune that befalls people:

❑ Suffering is sent by God to test us and make us stronger.

❑ God does not give people more burdens than they can bear.

❑ Sometimes bad things happen to good people, and that's just the way it happens.

❑ God does not necessarily "give" us suffering, but God is present to us when we suffer.

❑ When taken up in a spirit of faith, suffering can help a marriage grow stronger.

❑ Other: (write your own)

3. What practices, religious or otherwise, can you and your spouse do that will help you face the inevitable changes that will occur in your future?

4. Do you know of any couples who have endured the challenges of life, have "hung in there" through adversity, and become better people despite it all? What do you admire about them the most?

Case Study 1

Lauren and Rob have been married for six years. In that time they have had two children, now ages four and two. At the time they were courting Lauren was attracted to Rob's quiet demeanor, his sensitivity and his "laid-back" style. Nothing seemed to bother him. Rob was attracted to Lauren's independence, her love for sports and for the physically affectionate way she showed her appreciation and admiration for him. Now, six years into their marriage, Lauren and Rob found themselves fighting more and more. Both felt a bit betrayed because of the way things had changed. According to Rob, Lauren no longer showed him physical affection. At the same time, she complained about the demands of parenting two young children. When they argued she would sometimes criticize him. He felt pushed away by her. According to Lauren, Rob was no  longer "laid back" but intense in a way that she felt was parental toward her. He would criticize her for not having the house picked up. He also would complain about the lack of sexual contact. Their sexual frequency had dropped from two to three times a week to once every six weeks. Sometimes each would criticize the other, saying, "I sure wish I had known you were like this before we got married." Both still wanted the marriage to work but they didn't know how to get things back on track.

Reflecting Together

1. What do you think is the root problem for the couple in the case above? Do you think this is more of a case of the couple not knowing each other or of the effects of accumulated stress on the two of them?

2. In a case like this do you think that a separation is ever called for? If not, what would you advise this couple to do?

Case Study 2

Linda and Raymond have been married for three years. When they dated and became engaged they literally did everything together: they would meet after work for dinner, then either go to a movie or just take long walks. On other nights they participated in a mixed couples softball league. When Raymond played basketball, Linda would be there to watch. When Linda played volleyball, Raymond would be there to cheer her on. They had common interests and often stayed up until two to three a.m. talking by themselves or with friends.

Over the past year and a half things have slowly changed. Both of them got promotions at their jobs which required longer hours. They had less time to do things with each other after work. Linda sometimes had to go on the road and spend a night or two away from Raymond. On the weekends they found themselves so exhausted that they often slept late. Additionally, they continued to meet their old friends for drinks during the week and on the weekend. Both of them occasionally went to work with a hangover. The upshot was that they increasingly felt more tired and stretched.

One weekend the two of them had a long talk and both expressed dissatisfaction to what was happening to them. They decided to take advantage of Raymond's Employee Assistance Program and met with a marriage therapist. She was able to point out to them that they were both under more stress and that they were no longer doing as many things together that they really enjoyed doing. She challenged their practice of meeting friends for drinks and suggested that they needed to discover new behaviors and rituals that would renew their marriage. They left her office with the task to come up with a list of things, old and new, that would continue to build their relationship. But she gave them one condition: each item could not involve the consumption of alcohol or other drugs, for she wanted them to build their relationship without relying on alcohol.

Reflecting Together

1. Do you know of anyone who has experienced a scenario similar to the one above? How did they solve this problem?

2. Do you agree that married couples need to establish new behaviors and rituals that are different than the "single crowd?" Why or why not?

3. Do you have any concerns about how your partner handles stress and takes care of himself or herself? If yes, what would you want to see your fiancé do differently?

4. Are there any couples your age or slightly older who you would look to as models for weathering the more demanding changes that life sometimes throws our way?

5. Can you think of any crisis or significant change that affected your parent's marriage when you were growing up? How did each of your parents react? What did you learn from each of them about dealing with change?

Prayers for the Engaged and Newly Married Couple

For a Passionate, Creative Love

Lord, send out your Spirit
and renew the face of the earth.
Father, Jesus gave his life
because he loved deeply and completely.
May our love for one another
be all encompassing and all consuming.
Make our love be pleasurable.
Make it be creative as it is stable,
passionate as it is respectful,
gentle as it is strong,
so that all who know us will see in our
love the hand of our Creator God.
And when you bless us with children
may they grow in the knowledge of the
passionate and energizing love that
has its beginning in the love you have
for the world and all its peoples.
We ask this through Jesus, our Lord and brother.
Amen.

A Prayer for Understanding

Lord, help us to always seek first to understand each other,
to lead with compassion,
to walk a while in the other's experience.
Help us walk the road of marriage together,
trusting that when we doubt you will give us faith,
that when we criticize you will give us the courage to seek and give forgiveness.
Make our love for one another burn in our hearts
in tough times as well as in the easy times.
May your Spirit renew our love again and again
so that we may give witness to your saving presence in our lives.
Amen.

A Prayer for Perseverance

Lord Jesus, in the garden of Gethsemane
you did not want to face the pain you knew would happen to you.
Yet you persevered and did not run from
what lay ahead of you.
Guide us gently to face our fears.
Like your disciples in the storm-tossed boat
we sometimes feel swamped by life's indifferent pressures.
May your presence always comfort us and lead us beyond fear to hope.
Help us to develop confidence in our own skills;
let us face our future with confidence in your sustaining presence.
Amen.

A Prayer to Tobias and Sarah

Tobias and Sarah, pray for us as we begin a life together.
You risked your reputation and your lives
for the sake of your love for each other.
Keep us faithful to our own journey of love.
Guide us to do what is right, not what others say is right.
May we be helpmates and partners to each other
and may God's Spirit keep us single minded in our fidelity.
May your spirit teach us about energy and zeal for God's love;
as we walk our journey together may God's love always energize us.
Amen.

To Anna and Joachim: On Children

We pray that our children will reach their full potential in the eyes of God,
as did your daughter Mary,
mother of Jesus our Lord.
May God's Holy Spirit lead us in the way of wonder and love
so that when we become parents
we will provide a home full of care, comfort, and structure.
Teach us to be a family that is holy,
one that sees in every person the dwelling place for God's Spirit.
As you taught your daughter Mary,
teach us to value our children for who they are,
not so much for what they can do.
May God keep us always loving and present
to the many joys, struggles, and hopes that our children possess.
Amen.

For Forgiveness: A Prayer to St. Peter

Peter, who Jesus called Rock,
you know the pain and agony of having denied your friend and master.
Yet you were forgiven and called to mighty deeds.
Peter, you were married when Jesus called you to leave your nets and follow him.
Was your wife your silent partner?
Did she anchor you to reality when you dreamed wild schemes
and plans for the newborn church?
Did you have to seek her forgiveness for the excesses of your enthusiasm?
Pray for us, Rock of the church,
when we fail our commitments
and even betray our friendship with each other.
Help us see that beyond the hurt and pain lies the grace of renewal.
As Jesus forgave you
may we forgive each other and not harbor lasting resentment.
May our attitude always be as a child
who quickly forgets the hurt
because of the consoling presence of a loving friend.
We ask this through Jesus, our Lord and brother.
Amen.

A Prayer Concerning Conflict

Jesus, were there ever times when you became angry with your friends?
When you rebuked Peter and called him "Satan"
were you angry because he tried to control what you were saying?
Show us that conflict can be holy ground,
that it need not be destructive.
Keep us honest and respectful of each other when we fight.
Lead us to take responsibility for our words and actions.
Remind us that we can always do better,
especially if we hit below the belt by name calling and harsh criticism.
Above all else, send us your Spirit
to lead us in the way of respect and honesty,
so that our love may continue to deepen through the years.
Amen.

A Prayer to Abraham and Sarah

Abraham and Sarah, you risked all to journey to a new land you did not know.
And when you were old and beyond your child bearing years
God granted your wish for a son.
You dared to dream, to laugh, and to hope in the promise of God.
Pray for us as we begin our journey of love.
Give us some of your vision.
May our dreams be rooted in the passion, perseverance, and humor
that the two of you possessed.
May God always lead us into our future.
Amen.

To Sarah, on Laughter

When the angel announced to Abraham
that you would bear a son,
you laughed because you were old and beyond your years.
Yet God laughed with you and gave you Isaac.
We pray that our marriage be for us a place of safety and a place of mirth.
May God keep our commitment to one another strong
and our love ever growing.
May we be able to laugh at ourselves
and not take ourselves too seriously.
With the help of the Spirit
may we transcend our limitations and sinfulness.
As we grow older we pray that we, too,
can laugh and play in God's presence.
Amen.

The Covenant of Our Marriage

Father, you are creator of all things
and you renew our commitments even when we fail
to keep our end of the covenant we make with you.
Keep us faithful to the covenant we enter together.
Help us realize that your sustaining presence
will guide us through the tough times that we will face.
When we are tempted to turn away from each other
help us face our fears.
And when we want to blame the other for not meeting our needs
teach us to take responsibility for ourselves.
Help us celebrate and proclaim
the lasting quality of our commitment to each other,
so that in seeing our love
others may see your presence.
Amen.

The Prayer of All Christians

Our Father,
who art in heaven,
hallowed be thy name;
thy kingdom come;
thy will be done
on earth as it is in heaven.
Give us this day our daily bread;
and forgive us our trespasses
as we forgive those who trespass against us;
and lead us not into temptation,
but deliver us from evil.
Amen.